Prepare for the GPC Exam

Earn Your Grant Professional Certified Credential

Pauline Annarino, GPC

Danny W. Blitch II, GPC

Kimberly Hays de Muga, GPC

Leslie Mitchell, GPC

*Charity*Channel

PRESS

Prepare for the GPC Exam: Earn Your Grant Professional Certified Credential

One of the **In the Trenches™** series

Published by

CharityChannel Press, an imprint of CharityChannel LLC

424 Church Street, Suite 2000

Nashville, TN 37219 USA

CharityChannel.com

ISBN Print Book: 978-1-938077-84-5

Library of Congress Control Number: 2015957466

13 12 11 10 9 8 7 6 5 4 3 2

Printed in the United States of America

This and most CharityChannel Press books are available at special quantity discounts for bulk purchases for sales promotions, premiums, fundraising, or educational use. For information, contact CharityChannel Press, 424 Church Street, Suite 2000, Nashville, TN 37219 USA. +1 949-589-5938.

Publisher's Acknowledgments

This book was produced by a team dedicated to excellence; please send your feedback to Editors@ CharityChannel.com.

We first wish to acknowledge the tens of thousands of peers who call *CharityChannel.com* their online professional home. Your enthusiastic support for the **In the Trenches**™ series is the wind in our sails.

Members of the team who produced this book include:

Editors

Acquisitions: Linda Lysakowski

Organizing: Danny W. Blitch II

Manuscript: Deb Derrick and Stephen C. Nill

Production

Layout: Stephen Nill

Design: Deborah Perdue

Administrative

CharityChannel LLC: Stephen C. Nill, CEO

Marketing and Public Relations: John Millen

About the Authors

This book is a collaboration of grant, fundraising, editorial, and publishing professionals. The use of "we" implies our agreement with the final version of the book. That doesn't mean that agreement was always easy. As with any group writing project, some tough decisions were made to get this book into print. Grant professionals will be familiar with this group-editing process. As authors, we are proud of the collaborative results. We hope our readers, whether they're new to grants or seasoned grant veterans, find it helpful.

Pauline Annarino, GPC

Pauline Annarino, MS, NAD V, GPC is a graduate of the University of Wisconsin-Milwaukee. Her career has been split (as well as commingled) between deaf advocacy/sign language interpretation and grant development. She wrote her first grant in 1978. Since that time she has developed more than one hundred proposals in both the public and private sectors. Pauline was president of the Grant Professionals Association (GPA) from 2005 to 2008 and the Grant Professionals Certification Institute (GPCI) from 2004 to 2007. She was the lead architect of the Grant Professionals Certification (GPC). Pauline's work was recognized by GPCI, which established the Pauline G. Annarino Award for individuals who have made a public contribution to grantsmanship. She is passionate about elevating the grant field and looks forward to working "in the trenches" to promote the grantsmanship field and its ethical practices.

Danny W. Blitch II, GPC

Danny W. Blitch II is an original GPC, receiving the credential in 2008. He serves as the Grants Manager for the City of Roswell, Georgia, where he is responsible for a municipal grant program which has been awarded more than $65 million in grants. His career in grants includes experience at a municipality, a county board of education, a regional development center, a state university's development office, and as a grant development consultant. He has more than twenty years of experience with federal, state, and local government grants; private donations; fundraising; and project management. As a consultant, his work has produced more than $24 million in government grants for clients nationwide.

Danny is a frequent speaker, presenter, trainer, and author. He serves on several national and local nonprofit boards. He joined the Grant Professionals Foundation Board of Directors in 2007, and served as its chair from 2008-2011. He was instrumental in the creation of the groundbreaking Grant Professionals Impact Survey. He was also a director on the Grant Professionals Association Board of Directors from 2013 to 2015. During his board service he led the establishment of International Grant Professionals Day and the week-long celebration of the grant profession that occurs annually in March.

Kimberly Hays de Muga, GPC

Kimberly Hays de Muga, GPC is an expert in helping nonprofit professionals do well at doing good. She is the Development Director for the Frazer Center in Atlanta and a past president of the Georgia GPA chapter. Kimberly has raised millions of dollars from foundations and corporations for human service nonprofits for more than fifteen years, including mobile food pantries, interfaith children's camps, and general operating support for the largest pediatric hospital in the Southeast. Her passion is helping nonprofits and funders better connect through training and coaching—and ultimately help more people in need.

In the last five years, she has authored and coauthored two articles published in the *JGPA* and has presented regularly at GPA national conferences and at GPA regional conferences in Atlanta and Memphis.

Kimberly joined the GPF board in 2010. She is the current board chair and serves on the fundraising committee.

Leslie Mitchell, GPC

Leslie Mitchell, GPC has nearly thirty years of experience in nonprofit organizations in social services, education, mental health, and healthcare. Her undergraduate degrees are in mental health and business, and she holds a master's degree in business management. This background has provided her with rich experience she uses as a grant professional. Leslie has over fifteen years' experience in the grant field as a practitioner. She received her GPC with the inaugural class in 2008. She has served on several GPA national committees and is currently the chair of the Ethics Committee. Leslie is a board member of her local chapter.

Dedication

To all of my mentors and colleagues who saw merit in my work, and to the early pioneers of GPA, who saw merit in the field. And, of course, to my family, Paul, Bailey, and Bradley Westerhoff, who supported my career and the authoring of this book.

   — Pauline Annarino, GPC

Thank you to the women in my life, including my wife, Cynthia, and my mom, Patricia. Your belief in me makes my "grant" things possible!

   — Danny W. Blitch II, GPC

Many thanks to E for keeping the faith and maintaining "the estate" during a tumultuous writing process.

   — Kimberly Hays de Muga, GPC

To my lover, partner, and best friend, Michael. You believe in me far more than I do myself. Without your support, this would not have been possible.

   — Leslie Mitchell, GPC

Authors' Acknowledgments

The authors acknowledge the impressive and comprehensive work done by the fine folks at the Grant Professionals Certification Institute (GPCI). GPCI laid the foundation for the GPC credential and, in doing so, elevated our profession.

We would like to thank the gifted and talented team of professionals at CharityChannel Press! A book is merely a pile of double-sided pages until your work to print, advertise, and ship is done.

The editors have made a gargantuan process manageable. We appreciate Diane Sunden, our first and former comprehensive editor. Thank you, Diane, for giving us our initial footing and the ball to roll. Thank you, Stephen Nill, for agreeing to pick up the ball and carry it back to us through the darkness, only partially illuminated by the eerie computer screen glow of a dozen videos! Deb Derrick, we are grateful for your cheerful attention to the details as we huddled for the final publish push. And Linda Lysakowski, thanks for your thoughtful guidance, advice, and calm demeanor. We will never forget that you believed in us, and this project, before anyone else!

The competence of our peer reviewers cannot be overstated. Thank you all for seeing what we couldn't on our own and pushing us to define, refine, and solidify our beliefs. We thank all of you for your help, penetrating questions, and understanding the point and purpose of this book.

Our sincere thanks go to everyone at our places of work who overlooked our incessant grant jokes and to those who let us slide on our regular project assignments as we labored for love of the GPC.

Finally, we would like to thank the Oxford comma. It does make a difference!

Contents

Summary of Chapters

Grant Research. Grant research involves vetting grant announcements to determine if the call for proposals is appropriate for your organization, among other things. Ideally, this research process starts with a defined, well-designed program or project.

Organizational Development. Many nonprofit leaders and board members assume that because they're designated as a 501(c)(3) organization, they're ready to receive grant funding. Anyone can write proposals, of course, but it takes a lot more to show funders that your organization is grant ready.

Good Project Design. It takes a village, or at least a handful of people, to develop a new project or program. The ideal team includes the grant professional, project director, at least one direct staff member, someone from the finance department, and someone who is strong in program evaluation. Creating an effective team or plan is much easier than creating an effective, impactful project!

Grant Proposal Development. Grant development is more than just grant writing. It's a complicated capacity-building process. You need to understand the questions, components, documents, and financials needed and then build in enough time to gather the required data while also writing clearly, concisely, and compellingly.

Grant Postaward Management. Grant management is essentially doing what you said you would do in the grant proposal. Managing your grant projects properly is vitally important in maintaining relationships with current and future funders. Grant management isn't exciting to everyone, but it's an important responsibility for grant professionals.

Ethics. Having a strong ethical framework is an important part of any profession. The GPA Code of Ethics is the scaffolding on which our field is built. This chapter discusses the code of ethics, why ethical practice is important, and some common pitfalls that we face in our work.

Professional Practices. Grant professionalism is more than a critical definition, more than a skill, and more than a credential. Good habits are the foundation of professionalism. If you know your craft and are familiar with its rules and regulations, you have important and marketable skills.

Relationships! Relationships! Relationships! The best written proposal in the world can fall flat in today's super competitive funding arena without a connection to the program officer, board of trustees, or family member of a family foundation. Building working relationships and making meaningful connections over time is what helps a grant program grow—ultimately creating positive changes in the communities you serve.

The Writing Prompt. The GPC exam includes a writing exercise that is evaluated by GPCI. Your original essay must make a persuasive argument, be organized and clear, use the information provided in the writing prompt, adhere to conventional Standard English, and follow specific formatting requirements.

Strategies to Reduce Test Anxiety. The authors, who have all taken the exam, help you to reduce your anxiety about the exam. In this chapter, you'll find recommended reading, literature review and study lists, and resources for online test taking strategies to reduce test taking anxiety.

Foreword

The journey toward the *Prepare for the GPC Exam* guide you are now reading actually began five years ago when I chaired the Grant Professionals Foundation. I thought GPF was the perfect vehicle to deliver high-quality educational classes and webinars for people interested in taking the GPC exam. We could deliver the training, GPCI would have more certified grant professionals, and GPA would further cement its position as the authority on all things grants. It would be the greatest win-win of my grant career!

I reached out to several giants in the grant profession who'd spent so much of their careers giving back to the profession. Luckily, Pauline Annarino, Gail Widner, Leslie Mitchell, and Sandra Jordan agreed to join me in this important endeavor. We struggled for years to develop a top-notch curriculum and materials, an instructor selection application, and assessment procedures. Unfortunately, our profit margins were too low and difficult to predict. Our investors and the GPF board found my idea too expensive and too risky. Our approach wasn't going to work.

Several other groups and a couple of businesses had learned the hard way, too. They shared our excitement over the GPC credential, but quickly learned that a traditional education delivery model would have to change to be profitable. Then my ah-ha! moment happened. At a GPA conference in Florida, I heard Stephen Nill, Linda Lysakowski, and Amy Eisenstein speak about writing books for CharityChannel Press, the publishing arm of the CharityChannel professional community, and I knew what I had to do!

CharityChannel agreed to listen, and together, we put together an impressive team to write this manual.

As an editor and author, I've learned so much from this process. I would like to thank the other authors, their families and spouses, all of the editors, production professionals, and those who love them. I appreciate your willingness to share your time, skills, and abilities. The power of the group made this important project a reality.

The *Prepare for the GPC Exam* manual is happy to have found a home at CharityChannel Press. We are proud to be part of the In the Trenches family of titles for practitioners, by practitioners. The series makes sense for us on many levels. The GPC exam is for people with several years of successful grant experience. This manual is meant to help you register for the exam, explain the GPCI competencies, provide a skills refresher, prepare to do well on both the multiple-choice and written sections, and get up to speed on maintaining your GPC certification after you've got it.

I'm most proud of our plan to give back to the profession because it's served us all so well. A percentage of the proceeds from the sale of this manual established the Giving Back Scholarship Fund for GPC exam scholarships.

Thank you for choosing this manual. We trust you will find it helpful, whether you are interested in the grant profession, curious about what to expect if you're new to grants, or plan on taking the GPC exam one day.

—Danny W. Blitch II, GPC
    Organizing Editor and Coauthor

Introduction

If you've been writing grants for a while, or even if you're a newbie, you know that the competition for grant dollars is stiffer than ever. As a grant professional, you've got to keep up with the field and be "on your game" at all times. One of the ways to do this is to join a professional association like Grant Professionals Association (GPA). Another way to demonstrate your knowledge and competency in the grant field is to become certified.

If you're thinking of taking the Grant Professional Certified (GPC) examination, or want to know more about the grant field, this manual is for you! You may already know someone who's taken the exam and become certified. Maybe you've wondered what the exam was all about—what types of information are covered and what topics you may need to become more familiar with. This guide tells you all this and much more.

This manual is a comprehensive refresher-level look at the GPC exam. The exam is administered by GPCI. It tests you on the skills and competencies you need to have to perform well in the grant field. In order to "sit" for the GPC exam, you need to meet certain eligibility criteria. The GPC exam itself has two parts: a multiple-choice section and a written section. If you pass both sections, you'll receive the GPC credential for an initial period of three years. You'll then need to participate in continuing education to maintain the GPC credential and renew it every three years after passing the exam.

The GPC credential is highly sought-after by grant professional generalists. A grant professional generalist is someone who's mastered a wide range of grant-related knowledge and who has a deep understanding of grant programs, funding sources, opportunities, organizational development, and community collaboration. Grant professionals must exhibit a number of skills, especially the ability to write persuasively.

The topics in this manual are based on the *GPC Competencies and Skills* and are written for practitioners in the trenches as a refresher for the GPC exam. But students and early-career professionals can also learn about the grant profession from this manual. We've organized this manual into ten self-contained chapters, which include each of GPCI's nine competencies as well as a final chapter on strategies to reduce test anxiety.

GPCI's Validated Competencies

GPCI has established nine core competencies for the GPC credential. This process took more than seven years and involved three independent entities: GPCI, GPA (formerly, the American Association of Grant Professionals), and the University of Southern Florida. Many people in these three organizations

Are There Really *Nine* Validated Competencies? Sort of!

The Grant Professionals Certification Institute (GPCI) established eight competencies with sixty different skills, plus a set of six skills for the writing portion of the exam.

So, why do we refer to them as *nine* competencies? For purposes of this manual we refer to the eight competencies, together with the writing prompt's evaluation criteria, as nine competencies. We devote each of **Chapters One** through **Eight** to a "formal" competency—and **Chapter Nine** to the writing prompt.

Oh, and we threw in **Chapter Ten,** which gives you valuable tips designed to lower your anxiety about taking the exam.

observation

contributed their knowledge and expertise to identify the competencies and skills someone should have in order to be considered a certified grant professional. They worked together to create the GPC credential, develop and validate the examination questions and examination process, and secure accreditation from an external credentialing body.

The process included more than one hundred subject-matter experts and volunteers. Together, they came up with nine validated competencies. GPCI tests candidates on these competencies before conferring the GPC credential.

The GPC exam includes two sections, each of which must successfully be completed by the candidate. One is a writing exercise and the other is a multiple-choice exam.

The Multiple-choice Section

The multiple-choice section of the GPC exam includes 150 to 160 questions that are weighted to reflect the overall competencies and skills of each candidate within the profession.

The competencies and skills tested in this section, and the weight assigned to each, were determined through a rigorous process that involved the participation of numerous professionals, subject-matter experts, and the assistance of credentialing experts.

Each question is either a question or scenario with four possible responses. (In case there's any confusion here, only one answer is right.) The exam tests for knowledge of the following eight competencies, with the weight given for competency.

◆ Knowledge of how to research, identify, and match funding resources to meet specific needs (15 percent)

◆ Knowledge of organizational development as it pertains to grant seeking (10 percent)

◆ Knowledge of strategies for effective program and project design and development (20 percent)

◆ Knowledge of how to craft, construct, and submit an effective grant application (25 percent)

◆ Knowledge of postaward grant management practices sufficient to inform effective grant design and development (8 percent)

◆ Knowledge of nationally-recognized standards of ethical practice by grant developers (10 percent)

◆ Knowledge of practices and services that raise the level of professionalism of grant developers (4 percent)

◆ Knowledge of methods and strategies that cultivate and maintain relationships between fund-seeking and recipient organizations and funders (8 percent)

TOTAL: 100 percent

GPC candidates will have up to four hours to complete the multiple-choice portion of the exam. The multiple-choice exam is only available in an electronic format.

Competency versus Skill

A *competency* is a broad area of knowledge in a discipline or profession. A *skill* is the behavior that demonstrates that competency.

GPC Writing Prompt

The GPC exam includes a writing section. Sometimes this is referred to as the writing sample. The writing portion is designed to test your writing skills and your ability to follow directions. The writing prompt will include directions to follow, some critical details, and the specific type of writing GPCI is looking for from the applicant. The writing portion should be very familiar to applicants and is similar to the type of writing required of most grant applications.

Your writing must make a persuasive argument. It should also be organized and clear, use the information provided in the prompt, adhere to conventional Standard English, and follow the formatting requirements provided.

You have ninety minutes to complete the writing section of the GPC exam.

Writing a Convincing Case for Funding

The writing portion assesses your ability to craft a well-written, compelling response to a brief description or scenario. Don't worry! You can access a practice window before the exam to get used to the exam format and screen. Everyone uses the exact same format.

Your writing sample will be evaluated according to six skills that are key to successful grant development. These skills and their respective weights are listed below and form a composite writing score:

◆ Make a persuasive argument (34 percent)

◆ Organize ideas appropriately (22 percent)

◆ Convey ideas clearly (18 percent)

◆ Use information provided (12 percent)

◆ Use conventional Standard English (10 percent)

◆ Follow formatting requirements (4 percent)

TOTAL: 100 percent

The Value of the GPC Credential

Holding a GPC credential means more than having a set of initials after your name. It means that you've already achieved a lot—a lot of knowledge, experience, education, and involvement in your community. And you've put that knowledge and experience to the test by passing a rigorous examination.

Your GPC credential validates your knowledge of and competency in the grant profession through a psychometrically sound examination. The GPCI competencies are based on widely accepted sociological theories of the professionalization of careers, an extensive literature review, the expertise of highly experienced authorities in the grant field, and examination development processes of the American Psychological Association.

Think of it like the bar exam for lawyers, only directed toward the skills and experience needed to be a successful grant professional. A GPC isn't a certificate of completion. No one gets a GPC by paying for and sitting through a class or series of classes. It's based on experience and a wide body of knowledge and the ability to write clear and compelling grant communications under deadline pressure.

People often mistake a certificate of completion, or an assessment-based certificate, as a *professional certification* or credential.

The GPC is more than a certificate of attendance or an assessment-based certificate program. It's a credential or letters that should be proudly added after your name. A credential expresses mastery of a

---

What's the Difference?

The National Organization for Competency Assurance (NOCA) provides a clear distinction between a certificate of attendance or participation, assessment-based certificate, and a professional certification. NOCA is the leader in setting quality standards for credentialing organizations. Its division, the National Commission for Certifying Agencies, has provided more than thirty years of accrediting services to the credentialing industry. NOCA defines the three terms in the following way.

Certificates of Attendance or Participation

A Certificate of Attendance or Participation is given to those who have attended or participated in classes, courses, or other educational programs or events. It's meant to show that the participants have mastered the intended learning outcomes of the class or training. However, this mastery is *not* a requirement for receiving the certificate.

Assessment-based Certificate Programs

Assessment-based certificate programs are also valuable and, for the most part, the instructors are qualified to teach about grants. These programs are a step up from certificates of attendance, but again, they do not confer actual credentials. They evaluate participants' accomplishment of the intended learning outcomes, and award a certificate only to those who meet the performance, proficiency, or passing standard for the assessments. Hence the term *assessment-based* certificate program.

Professional Certification

Professional certifications provide a time-limited recognition and use of a credential to those who have demonstrated that they have met predetermined and standardized criteria for required knowledge, skills, or competencies. They primarily focus on assessment of predetermined standards for knowledge, skills or competencies, rather than assessment of the learning outcomes of a particular education or training program. If you have a professional certification, you can use that credential or letters following your name, indicating that you have satisfactorily met the requirements for certification.

observation

field of study. Many grant training programs are a collection of classes or several related courses. Some places offer the training free of charge, such as federal agencies, and some businesses even provide a paper certificate for participation. A few even administer a test after the class. There's value in these classes, but they cannot be construed as a credential.

The GPC is a professional certification or credential. The credential is officially conferred and allows recipients to use the letters after their name, for example, "Danny W. Blitch II, GPC."

GPCI created the GPC credential following a standardized process, administers a Certification Maintenance Program, and enforces sanctions for ethical violations. The credential is psychometrically valid and fully accredited.

When you see the terms *certificate* or *certification* bantered about in marketing materials, take a moment to figure out if they are referring to a certificate of completion, an assessment-based certificate tied to a particular training, or a professional certificate. And remember: a certificate of attendance or completion states that an individual has completed a class or course and achieved a certain level of success in understanding the principles taught in the course. A professional certification or credential is an objective measure of a person's level of experience and expertise in the profession—as defined independently by the profession as a whole.

Why Provide a GPC Skills Refresher?

As grant professionals, we share a common set of skills such as clear writing, budgeting expertise, and strong organizational skills. But we bring these skills and abilities to very different environments. A corporate and foundation grant specialist may want to brush up on federal grant regulations. A consultant specializing in preparing federal and state grants may want to review cultivation and reporting concepts. This manual reviews these key concepts and is useful to those seeking to balance out their overall knowledge.

The GPC exam costs time and money. Some folks might consider it wasteful to take the exam without reviewing the exam material and brushing up on their grant-related skills.

Grant Writers versus Grant Professionals

The question, "What is the distinction between grant writers and grant professionals?" comes up occasionally. Honestly, the terms are often used interchangeably. Most people prefer the term "grant professional" because it better represents the work we do. The term "grant writer" is limiting because the profession involves so much more than writing.

A grant writer drafts language for proposals and grant applications which are then reviewed by a supervisor and/or a review committee. A grant professional, on the other hand, may be a writer, project designer, program implementer, project reporter, or project manager. A grant professional may also be responsible for financial oversight, audit, and closeout of the grant. Some grant professionals prefer to be called "grant developers."

A GPC exam prep manual is important for a number of reasons. It may have been a long time since you've taken a timed exam. In addition, not all grant professionals are generalists when it comes to knowledge of grants—some are highly specialized. Whether you're a specialist or generalist, this manual will help you brush up on the core skills and knowledge you need to take and pass the GPC exam. If you're working in the trenches, you can benefit the most from an internationally-recognized credential.

And the more GPCs conferred by GPCI, the stronger the grant profession.

The GPC exam is a generalist test designed for an individual who demonstrates mastery and experience. It is not an entry-level exam. Anyone taking the GPC exam should not have to spend a great deal of time studying or preparing. However, studying and reviewing materials may be helpful if you specialize in one area (that is, you only write federal proposals and not foundation proposals) and need to enhance your knowledge in other areas.

What Was Your Major?

There is no one generally-preferred degree for grant professionals. Until very recently, few colleges and universities offered concentrations or degrees specific to the grant profession.

observation

Who Is Eligible to Take the Exam?

Anyone who has a minimum of three years of grant experience gained in the last five years, a track record of success in obtaining grant funding, professional development, postsecondary education, and/or community and volunteer work is eligible to take the GPC exam.

Grant Experience

Experience in the grant profession is measured in years. Your experience doesn't have to be consecutive, but it does need to be relevant. Your grant experience should be within the last five years prior to the date you register to take the exam. Your work in the grant profession can be either as an employee or as a professional consultant.

Grant Awards

Grants are awarded most often to organizations rather than individuals. GPCI considers grant award experience to be based on the number of funded grant proposals you've been responsible for developing in the seven-year period prior to your registration date. The minimum requirement is five grant awards or more in the past seven years.

Professional Development and Other Work

You must show that you've met at least two of the following three criteria: professional development, postsecondary education, and/or community and volunteer work. GPCI considers these three professional activities when evaluating and scoring a candidate's eligibility packet.

GPCI Eligibility Questionnaire

Candidates for the GPC exam complete a five-minute online survey to quickly assess whether they are likely to be eligible to sit for the exam. This process helps you make sure that you don't waste your time by completing a full eligibility packet unnecessarily.

The final page of the survey provides directions on the next steps, including payment of the exam registration fee.

The GPCI eligibility questionnaire includes three questions. The first is, "What is your level of education?" The three possible responses are:

◆ No college degree

◆ Associate's degree

◆ Bachelor's degree or higher

Answer honestly; there's no wrong answer here.

The second question is, "How many professional development activities have you completed in the past two years?" The response choices range from zero to four or more. Carefully read the eligibility criteria on the GPCI website for the definition of professional development and answer the question honestly. You may also want to check out the *GPC Examination Candidate Guide* available on the GPCI website.

The third question is, "How many community involvement activities have you participated in within the past two years?" The response choices range from zero to two or more. The GPCI website covers these definitions. Again, answer the question honestly according to these specific criteria.

Competencies and Skills

The GPC exam is based on the competencies and skills developed and continually updated by subject-matter experts within the grant field. The GPC credential is intended to give your employer or clients a level of confidence in your skills and grant knowledge. We realize that not all grant professionals are created equal, but the GPC is meant to provide an objective measuring stick of grant professionals for hire.

If you're approved by GPCI to sit for the examination, you'll receive an exam packet for review. We recommend that you fully review it, as well as the skills listed in this refresher manual, as both sources provide valuable insight into the competencies and types of questions on the exam.

How to Get the Most out of This Manual

This manual is divided into ten chapters and will cover the nine competencies tested by the GPC exam in **Chapter One** through **Chapter Nine,** plus an extra "insiders" chapter, **Chapter Ten,** "Strategies to Reduce Test Anxiety." Also, be sure to check out **Appendix A**, which has our recommended reading, and **Appendix B,** which refers you to the GPCI Literature Review.

Each chapter is written by an expert GPC grant professional. We've been in the trenches for decades and have learned most of what we know about grants on the job. We're sharing their knowledge with you and, in doing so, we're paying it forward by strengthening the grant profession. And, through an agreement with CharityChannel Press, we're also donating part of the proceeds from each manual sale toward scholarships for the GPC exam.

We also host blogs through CharityChannel Press, where we answer your questions and share our knowledge. These blogs offer another opportunity for you to get a "step ahead" of the competition.

Partnership with CharityChannel Press

CharityChannel Press is the publishing imprint of the CharityChannel professional community. Our community is made up of tens of thousands of busy, in-the-trenches practitioners who value these professional resources to help us achieve excellence in our day-to-day work for and on behalf of nonprofit organizations. CharityChannel Press is a trusted publishing house and a gathering place for many of the sector's most accomplished practitioners who are willing to give back by sharing their knowledge. We are proud to be a part of this community.

Giving back to the grant profession is not only the right thing to do, it's also a good business decision. CharityChannel Press has structured the publishing agreement to maximize the royalties for the authors and editors, and provide a sustainable manner in which the GPF will offer GPC exam scholarships on an annual basis based on manual sales proceeds.

Giving Back Scholarships

We have established the Giving Back Scholarship fund. A percentage of the proceeds will fund GPC exam scholarships.

CharityChannel Press will sell copies of the manual directly to GPA and GPF at a 20 percent discount, enabling these organizations to earn income on the sales. In addition, CharityChannel Press will provide Tier 2 Royalties of 20 percent to each of these organizations, implemented with a coded URL and periodic coupon codes, and work with them to market the manual. According to the NOCA accrediting standards, the GPCI cannot sell or accept proceeds from the sale of the manual.

Paying It Forward by Giving Back!

CharityChannel Press is partnering with the authors of this book to give back to the grant profession. We're donating a percentage of sales to the GPF for scholarships to take the GPC exam.

observation

Launching the GPC Credential and Online Exam

Hundreds of grant professionals took various forms of a pilot test and provided invaluable feedback on how to improve the questions. Two panels of experts, one in Portland, Oregon, and one in Washington, DC, convened to rewrite, refine, and in some cases replace test items. This process culminated in final test items and cutoff scores. Registration for the first examination launched in July, 2007. On November 10-11, 2007, over one hundred individuals sat for the first GPC exam in Arlington, Virginia.

In 2012, GPCI moved from a paper-based multiple-choice question exam and computer-based writing prompt to a full online examination. Today, you can take the GPC exam at nearly 700 Kryterion Testing Centers. Kryterion manages a "global network of High-stakes Online Secured Testing (HOST) locations through strategic partnerships with professional organizations such as colleges and universities, and testing and training companies." For a list of locations visit Kryterion's website at *kryteriononline.com*.

How Many GPCs Are There?

Since 2008, GPCI has conferred nearly 350 GPC credentials.

observation

After you complete the online survey at the registration site, you will be directed to a payment link to submit the exam registration fee.

Eligibility Packet

Following the receipt of the exam registration fee, you'll receive explicit instructions on submitting your GPC eligibility packet. Those who submit their packets by specific cohort dates and are approved to take the exam will have six months to schedule and take the exam.

Packet Approval

Your eligibility packet will be reviewed by at least three peer reviewers based on a scoring rubric established by the GPCI Board of Directors. You can expect to receive your approval within thirty days of the cohort submission deadline. For example, if the deadline is August 15, you should receive your approval by September 15. Generally, approval is within ten business days of the deadline.

Exam Voucher

Within seventy-two hours after your packet is approved, you'll receive a voucher number to reserve a seat for the GPC exam in a testing facility on a date of your choosing.

Site and Date Selection

You may choose to take both the multiple-choice and essay/writing portions of the exam at one time or you may stagger the sessions. However, both sections of the exam must be completed within the six-month period.

Certification Maintenance Program

A Grant Professional Certified (GPC) credential is valid for three years from the official date of acceptance. To maintain your certification, you must either satisfy the minimum training, volunteer, and job experience requirements outlined on the GPCI website and pay the certificate maintenance fee every three years, or retake the exam.

Most certified grant professionals choose to document their continuing education, publishing, grant-related service, and other activities rather than retake the GPC exam. Within three years from the certification date, you must earn a minimum of 105 points of professionally related activities in two or more professional development categories. In most but not all cases, one hour of professional development is assigned one Certification Maintenance Program (CMP) point.

There are five professional development categories from which you can earn points. These categories include education, grant employment, grant professional performance, professional service, and independent projects. Information regarding the CMP is located in the GPCI *CMP Manual*.

We recommend you keep a file of your grant-related continuing education, publishing, community service, and other activities to document the information needed for your CMP. Keeping a file as you go makes the process of gathering the information needed for your CMP much easier rather than waiting until a month before the paperwork is due.

> ### What's the GPC Exam Fee?
>
> As of going to press with this manual, the GPC exam registration fee is $539 for GPA members and $739 for non-GPA members. Be sure to check the GPCI website for updated pricing when you're ready to register.
>
> **observation**

> ### What's the CMP Fee?
>
> The GPC CMP Fee for 2015 is $180 for GPA members and $305 for non-GPA members. The 2015 penalty fees for submission of the application past the expiration due date, but prior to expiration of the three-month grace period, are $100 for GPA members and $150 for non-GPA members.
>
> **observation**

Grant Professionals Association

The Grant Professionals Association (GPA) is an international, professional membership association based in Overland Park, Kansas (USA). The GPA Board of Directors sets policies and procedures for governance of the association. The primary function of the association is member services and professional development at the GPA annual conference. The GPA conference is attended by approximately seven hundred members and nonmembers each year.

GPA serves members in forty-three chapters in twenty-nine states, Canada, and Puerto Rico. GPA member services include:

- Educational webinars

- A consultant directory

- Membership discounts

- Networking opportunities

- Committee and volunteer assignments

- Board and leadership work

- Access to resource tool kits and members-only materials

- Regional grant conferences

- GPA-approved trainers and GPA-endorsed businesses/ organizations

- Salary survey results

- Other surveys (consultant salary, membership, etc.)

- The *Journal of the Grant Professionals Association*

- Strategy papers

- GPA weekly e-blast

- Conference presentations and workshops

GPA Membership Growth 2003-2015

Active Grant Professionals Association Members	
2015	2,128
2014	1,973
2013	1,811
2012	1,823
2011	1,723
2010	1,674
2009	1,705
2008	1,537
2007	1,478
2006	1,194
2005	941
2004	700
2003	281

Source: Grant Professionals Association, Membership Update, December, 2015

observation

Who are the GPA Members?

According to the GPA website, "GPA has a growing international and affiliate chapter membership of over two thousand active members, all of whom have an interest in the grant profession. GPA members come from all sectors of the international grants community. They represent education, government, the nonprofit sector and private enterprise. They include grant developers, managers, funders, administrators, planners and evaluators. All promote and support the mission and philosophy of the association."

More information can be found on the GPA website at *grantprofessionals.org.*

The Grant Professionals Certification Institute

The Grant Professionals Certification Institute (GPCI) is the credentialing arm of GPA. GPCI (commonly informally pronounced "gypsy") is an independent board organized under the Internal Revenue Code as a 501(c)(3) nonprofit organization. GPCI administers the GPC credential and the CMP recertification process.

GPCI is dedicated to strengthening the nonprofit sector's ability to pursue and maintain public and private sector funding by promoting competency and ethical practices for grant professionals. It does so by identifying grant professionals who display outstanding expertise and ethical practices as measured by a psychometrically valid and reliable assessment tool.

Who Are the GPCs?

The broader answer to this question is that GPCs are grant professionals who have passed the GPC exam. Their experience, education, and background vary greatly, but collectively they're the experts of the grant profession. GPC grant professionals are working in nearly every state as well as internationally. GPC credential holders are employees and consultants. At least one is a publisher—Stephen Nill, CEO of CharityChannel Press, the publisher of this manual, has been a GPC since it was first offered. GPCI maintains a list of GPCs on its website at *grantcredential.org.*

Continuing Education, Too?

Those holding the GPC credential must participate in ongoing continuing education classes and grant-related professional activities, and recertify every three years to maintain their credential.

important

Grant Professionals Foundation

Grant Professionals Foundation (GPF) advances the grant profession by supporting local chapters, educational webinars, committee and volunteer assignments, board and leadership work, regional grant conferences, the Grant Professionals Impact Survey, grant research, other survey results, white papers, the monthly e-blast, and presentations, webinars, and workshops. The foundation is organized as a 501(c)(3) organization under the Internal Revenue Code.

GPF raises money to support scholarships, research, and other activities to advance the grant profession. It also raises funds for GPA conference scholarships, GPA membership scholarships, and GPC exam scholarships. These funds come from annual gifts from foundation board members, GPA members, corporations, and individuals.

Learn more by visiting the GPF website at *grantprofessionalsfoundation.org.*

Are You Exam Ready?

Each chapter in this manual includes a final section called "Are You Exam Ready?" You can assess your readiness to take the GPC exam by answering some essential questions.

You are exam ready if you:

◆ Are familiar with GPCI's nine validated competencies

◆ Know why a GPC skills refresher manual is available

◆ Know about CharityChannel's CharityUniversity online refresher course

◆ Know how to get the most out of this manual

◆ Know about the Giving Back Scholarships

◆ Know what to do to register for the GPC online exam

◆ Are familiar with the Grant Professionals Association

◆ Are familiar with the Grant Professionals Certification Institute

◆ Are familiar with the Grant Professionals Foundation

Chapter One

Grant Research

IN THIS CHAPTER

····➤ Identifying major trends in grant funding

····➤ Identifying funding sources and creating tracking systems

····➤ Identifying fundable programs and projects for organizations

····➤ Interpreting RFP guidelines and requirements

Let's get started by reviewing the first of nine GPCI competencies: "Knowledge of how to research, identify, and match funding resources to meet specific needs."

Without credible and legitimate grant opportunities, the best grant professional in the world would waste away in a cubicle somewhere, unappreciated and forgotten. Knowing where to find appropriate funding sources to match the funding needs of a given organization is as challenging as developing fundable projects. In other words, success in the gentle art of matchmaking between the funder and the grant-seeking organization is essential!

But the process doesn't end once a potential funding match is found. Assessing a funding opportunity helps clearly and precisely identify the funder's needs and focus areas. Not every request for proposals (RFP) is right for even a qualified organization to meet. You must realize that saying "no" to a proposal development opportunity now might mean saying "yes" to a larger award or better match in the next grant cycle. By not keeping up with trends in foundation or federal giving, or by losing touch with current donors, you may be leaving money on the table when it comes to funding opportunities. Grant research involves many skills and abilities. Like all research, it can take many hours, days, and sometimes months.

Grant Opportunity Research

So, you should be a shrewd matchmaker. Finding the right funding source and matching the grant opportunity to the correct organization is a critical skill every grant professional should have. Grant opportunity research is known by many names: grant research (or grant search), funding source research, or enormous time suck! For our purposes, grant research is the act of seeking legitimate grant funding sources and announcements and matching those opportunities up with "fundable" programs and projects. Fundable also means that the organization applying for the funds is *eligible* to apply.

If you're a successful grant professional, you know about the many different ways to search for funding opportunities. For starters, you can use paid subscription services, free search engines, government announcements and registers, and funders' websites. Local and university libraries often provide free access to pricier search engines. Your board members, business and community leaders, colleagues, and friends are all potential sources of useful funding leads. In addition, looking at annual reports and donor walls at other organizations can give you great information on who's funding programs similar to yours.

The Chicken or the Egg?

What comes first in grant research—the project needing funding or the grant opportunity? Ideally, a project is fully developed and understood before you seek funding. But sometimes the right funding opportunity is a chance to package related programs and services into a fundable project that meets the requirements of a specific funding opportunity. It's a chicken or egg kind of question. Or, sometimes food for thought can just make you hungry.

food for thought

Twisting the arms of internal staffers and interns and volunteers to pitch in is a time-honored tradition in grant research. So is hiring consultants to more proactively assess and connect projects with grant funding. And who hasn't spent hours on the Internet poring over 990s and chasing down contact information for their favorite celebrities…er…, focusing on grant research, of course!

There's no doubt that researching past funders and seeking the advice of colleagues and coworkers are key to overall grant research efforts as well. But beware of pawning off too much of your research to interns or coworkers if they're not trained in grant research. They may find too many opportunities that aren't appropriate for your needs. They can also miss some key prospects if they're not paying attention. You *must* train your helpers if you want to truly reduce your workload.

Which Comes First—Grant Opportunity or Funding Need?

Your project idea or need should serve as your guide. Keep it firmly in mind as you begin your research. You may discover few grant opportunities that directly match your project, your geographic focus, and/or your target population. Reconsidering your project or search criteria can lead your grant research into what grants are available by type, dollars awarded, geographic area benefit, or ideas most likely to get funded.

Beware the Illegitimate Funding Source

Illegitimate funding sources are crafty and try to look like legitimate ones. We've all run across examples of illegitimate funding sources; for example, a vendor may be reportedly giving away grants to potential buyers of its product. Now why would the vendor give away its product? One reason is that these grants often come in the form of "discounts," so the vendor is making money on the sale of the products.

Another example is the scammer who offers "free" services to clients who buy their product. The scammer will offer free grant writing services to anyone who will apply for funding and name their product specifically in the grant proposal, despite the fact that writing a specific product into a grant proposal harms the competitive procurement process. Regardless of what any late-night infomercial may promise, there's no such thing as free money!

watch out!

Be careful about inventing whole new programs just to match a few grant opportunities. For a truly well-designed program that meets definite and pressing needs of a given population, other types of funding could be an option. On the other hand, a well-meaning program or service that lacks defined goals or best practice activities may just be a nonstarter for grant funding. In other words, all good program ideas aren't fundable at all times. It takes a good mix of sound program structure and strategic prospect research to make a match.

Searching for Grant Opportunities

Successful grant research leads to finding more grant opportunity announcements and preparing more grant applications, leading to more grant awards for the benefit of more people, places, and things.

The keys to successful grant research include knowing where to look and knowing what you're looking for. When you research grants, you're looking for an active grant announcement from a reputable funding source or a foundation that has priorities that fit or align with your program. The application deadline needs to be realistic in terms of your project or program, and the focus of the grant opportunity needs to be relevant.

Although doing grant research for the sake of research can be productive, some would consider this type of research to be counter-productive. Knowing the grant universe or marketplace of grant opportunities would seem to be a good thing, but this isn't always the case. For example, "chasing the grant dollars" can lead to target population focus issues and the dreaded organizational mission creep. Chasing money is the practice of adjusting your programs to fit available requests for proposals instead of looking for funders to match your programs. Because chasing the dollars could become difficult to reign in later on, we believe it's best to avoid doing so.

If you ask yourself what the beneficiaries of your program or project *need*, you'll do the kind of research that gets better results in the long term. Overall, if you focus on the needs of the people (or animals) your organization serves or is attempting to serve, you'll have more success. Remember: the need is *not* for your organization (for more staff members, better computers, and so on). The need is for the betterment of the community or your target population, such as improving literacy, increasing graduation rates, or reducing response time in emergency situations. We'll discuss this further in **Chapter Four**.

Looking at the long-term impacts of your grant research will give you some important information on trends in policy and action. This information will help you predict the timing of funding announcements that may fit your programs. Knowing the potential funding sources for your organization and the people you serve will allow you to match up the grant opportunities you find with the programs and projects your organization has a track record of implementing. You'll be able to more easily spot new grant opportunities and evaluate them in support of your mission or organizational purpose.

What's a Grant Opportunity?

A grant opportunity, also commonly referred to as a Notice of Funding Announcement (NOFA) or an RFP, is a formal, written announcement of the type of funding offered, deadlines, and requirements. Generally, NOFAs are associated with federal or public funders and RFPs are released by smaller or private foundations.

Think of it like a job announcement. When a funder issues an RFP, they're seeking the best (of the best) grant proposals—just like an employer seeking to fill a job vacancy. After reading the grant application package, which is a lot like a job description, you should have an idea of the types of projects the funder is interested in supporting.

Just like a personal job search, grant opportunity research should be careful and considered. You want to match your skills, abilities, and interests as closely as possible with a potential employer. The same holds true for grant opportunities. Unless, of course, your idea of a good time is to waste weeks in futile grant preparation while receiving rejection after rejection. Then this manual and the grant profession may not be for you!

A grant application is also an opportunity for you to surprise the funder with a grant proposal that changes the grant landscape for them, for example, innovatively addressing critical needs for the benefit of more people.

Once an RFP or NOFA is published, the proposal deadline may be only weeks away. A few weeks are not enough time to create a research-based, well developed program or project worthy of being funded. And if you're lucky (or unlucky) enough to receive funding for a poorly planned or managed project, the reporting results alone could sour relations with a well-intentioned funder for years to come.

Ideally, the grant research process shouldn't start with a grant opportunity, but sometimes it does. We're all guilty of reacting quickly to a grant opportunity someone emailed to us. We scan the grant application and immediately start the internal grant approval process. We contact the program staff, agency supervisors, community partners, volunteers, and our favorite writers. The grant development process is at full steam, and then someone asks, "Why are we applying for this one?" The answer should always be, "because we did our homework and determined that this grant opportunity is perfect for us." The answer should never be, "I got this email and decided to wing it because I love deadlines."

Of Course, a Funding Source!

When looking for a grant, a past funding source might be a great place to start. You may know the trustees or the program officers and believe that your organization will always be a great applicant for their funding.

Be careful of assuming too much and thinking that the grant announcement rules don't apply to you. Making assumptions based on past experience with a funding source, or its grant application materials, can lead to a rejected proposal or professional embarrassment. A funding source can and will change the parameters of the grant proposals it's seeking from one grant round to the next. Read the grant application materials at least twice and take some notes on anything new before you claim that you know the grant guidelines "inside and out." Making decisions about a funding source's intent without doing your homework can lead to a lot of wasted time and bad decisions that ultimately keep your programs from serving the community. Of course, it's always best to check in with your program officer with any questions. We'll talk more about relationships in **Chapter Eight.**

Celebrated reporters Bob Woodward and Carl Bernstein broke the story of the Watergate scandal that toppled Richard Nixon's presidency by heeding a source's advice to "follow the money." For grant professionals, it makes sense to follow the money that was previously awarded and to understand what kind of money helped establish a grantmaking organization or agency.

But there's little need to meet anonymous sources in dimly lit parking garages to learn more about a potential funder, like in the Woodward and Bernstein days. Websites for foundations and government agencies often list past organizations and projects they funded and for how much. Online sites such as *guidestar.org* and *foundationcenter.org* compile thousands of 990 forms, which are the required tax documents for foundations that list grantees, boards of directors, and application instructions. Unfortunately, 990s can be many pages long, so make sure to schedule enough time and regular caffeine intake to slog through them.

Depending on the type of grant opportunity and funder, it may be possible to call the trustee or program officer directly for more information after you've completed some basic research. Doing your homework upfront on the funder and the kinds of programs they support will save you a lot of work in the long run.

The source of funding for government grantmakers can often be traced to an act of Congress, especially a budget allocation. Many federal grant opportunities are repeated from cycle to cycle. To research these funders, it's best to go to the federal department directly. Each department website will have upcoming opportunities as well as contact information for the individuals you can contact for more information.

> ### Where's the Money?
>
> Infamous bank robber William "Willy" Sutton was once asked by reporter Mitch Ohnstad why he robbed banks. Willy replied by saying, "Because that's where the money is." Don't let a notorious life of crime be your guide to successful grantsmanship. Get out there and find the right and legal kind of funding opportunities.
>
>

For example, if your organization is seeking funding for a mentoring program, you may want to visit the websites for the Department of Education or the Department of Justice. You'll find more subdepartments under each of these large departments that focus on mentoring. Follow their work and sign up for their email newsletters. That way, you'll be one of the first to know when a funding opportunity is released. The bonus is that they'll often have helpful toolkits that can make your current programs run more effectively.

Family foundations may emerge from the fortunes established several generations back, from a more recent initial public offering (IPO), or through the sale of a company. These funders often have regular funding cycles, which will help you plan the timing of your application or proposal writing. The websites of these funders will clue you in to what types of projects they will support.

Like a great matchmaker, you should carefully consider the qualities of the program or project in need of funding with the interests and requirements of the potential funder. An organization that changes its mission, target audience, and even core values to chase after funding dollars is not a grant research match made in heaven, or a chance for the community you serve to live "happily ever after."

Major Trends in Public Funding and Policy

Identifying major trends in public funding and public policy is both an art and a science. Several US government agencies publish information that is accessible to the public, and most of the federal grantmaking agencies provide public funding information. They all use the Internet and social media to educate the public on matters regarding public funding and public policy. This information is available on the federal grant website at *grants.gov.*

A great place to start research into public funding is the Office of Management and Budget (OMB). The OMB leads the development of government-wide policy to assure that grants are managed in accordance with applicable laws and regulations. The OMB website, at *http://whitehouse.gov/omb*, contains information about a number of focus areas that may receive government grants. These areas include civil rights, disabilities, economy, education, energy and environment, ethics, homeland security, seniors and Social Security, taxes, technology, urban and economic mobility, veterans and military families, violence prevention, and women. Read about the pertinent issues before you craft your proposal to the federal government. The OMB also provides links to presidential actions, such as executive orders, presidential memoranda, and proclamations.

The OMB does not award grants. To find the information necessary to apply for a federal grant, consult the Catalog of Federal Domestic Assistance (CFDA), which provides a short summary of each grant program and contact information for federal agencies that award grants.

Federal Grantmaking Agencies

There are many federal grantmaking agencies; most provide public funding information on an individual agency basis.

Catalog of Federal Domestic Assistance

The CFDA has detailed program descriptions for more than two thousand federal assistance programs. The CFDA website, at *cfda.gov,* provides a full listing of all federal programs available to state and local governments (including the District of Columbia); federally recognized Indian tribal governments; territories (and possessions) of the United States; domestic public, quasi-public, and private profit and nonprofit organizations and institutions; specialized groups; and individuals.

Trends in Public Funding

Public and/or government grant funding comes from the same place: taxpayers. Federal income tax dollars are the source of most federal grant-funded programs in the United States. To a large degree, the budget authorized by Congress and signed into law by the president is the source of public funding, including grants in this country. Federal-level agencies make the funds available in formula grants to the fifty states, tribes, and territories as well as to foreign countries. The states and territories make a portion of those funds available to county or city government agencies.

Other sources of information about public funding are, in fact, funded by the public. American taxpayers spend over $100 million a year to fund the Congressional Research Service (CRS), a "think tank" that provides reports to members of Congress on a variety of topics relevant to current political events. Unfortunately, these reports aren't made available to the public in a way that they can be easily obtained. Open CRS (Congressional Research Service Reports for the People) provides public access to CRS reports that are already in the public domain.

The Open CRS, at *opencrs.com,* is a good resource for grant professionals. CRS reports don't become public until a member of Congress releases the report. A number of libraries and nonprofit organizations have sought to collect as many of the released reports as possible. Open CRS is a centralized resource that brings these reports together.

Grants.gov is a US government website. It's used by grantors and grantees to find and apply for competitive grant opportunities from most federal grantmaking agencies. Many federal grant applications are submitted electronically through this website. *Grants.gov* also has many application tips and guidelines for filling out forms and submitting a successful application.

USA Spending is a website required by the Federal Funding Accountability and Transparency Act (FFATA). Check out the USA Spending website at *usaspending.gov.* The purpose of the legislation is to provide the public with information on how its tax dollars are spent. Collecting data about the various types of contracts, grants, loans, and other types of spending in our government provides a broader picture of the federal spending processes and helps meet the need for greater transparency. The ability to look at contracts, grants, loans, and other types of spending across many agencies, in greater detail, is a key ingredient to building public trust in government.

Trends in Public Policy

Public policy changes all the time. Congress passes (or doesn't pass) legislation that becomes federal public policy on grants. Each session of Congress is unique. It's important for grant professionals to be aware of these governmental actions because they affect funding streams and funding levels within government agencies. An example is reducing or increasing the amount of funding of a program like Medicare.

> ### Grantees and Grantors
>
> The *grantor* awards funds to the *grantee*, which is most commonly a nonprofit organization, educational institution, or state/local organization.
>
>

The following is an overview of public policy at the federal level. Each of the fifty states and the six US territories has separate public laws, regulations, and decisions. Read the content on credible websites before seeking grant policy information elsewhere.

The Office of Management and Budget

Working cooperatively with grantmaking agencies and the grantee community, the Office of Management and Budget (OMB) leads the development of government-wide policy to assure that grants are managed properly and that federal dollars are spent in accordance with applicable laws and regulations.

The OMB publishes public policy circulars that cover nearly every topic pertinent to federal agencies and funding. These circulars are relevant to proposal writing because the OMB lists certain criteria for projects that may receive public funding. For example, if you're writing a proposal for a project that will require staff members to attend training out of town, the OMB sets the rates at which you can add travel costs to your project budget. If the OMB says you can only reimburse mileage at fifty cents per mile, then you can't add a higher amount to your project budget.

The OMB circulars include policy that pertains to budget, state, and local governments, educational and nonprofit institutions, federal procurement, federal financial management, and federal information resources and data collection, among others.

> ### Public Policy
>
> Public policy is an attempt by a government to address a host of public issues by instituting laws, regulations, decisions, or actions pertinent to issues and problems at hand. Numerous issues can be addressed by public policy including crime, education, foreign affairs, health, and social welfare. While public policies are most common in the United States, several other countries, such as those in the United Kingdom, implement them as well.
>
>

Major Trends in Private Grant Funding

Private grant funding includes grantmaking foundations and corporations. A number of private companies provide data on private grant funding trends. As you can imagine, this kind of funding can be more complicated. There are millions of dollars in private grant funds disbursed each year from tens of thousands of foundations.

According to the Foundation Center, there was $24 billion in grant funding awarded from over 149,000 foundations in 2011. You can find more information on funding trends on its website at *http://data.foundationcenter.org*. There's a tremendous variety in the amounts awarded and in the requirements of each of these foundations. This is why private funding can be more challenging to navigate.

Of course, there are other credible sources besides the Foundation Center for information on nonprofit organizations. For example, the National Center for Charitable Statistics (NCCS), a project of the Urban Institute, conducts research and reports on information important to nonprofit organizations. According to the NCCS Business Master File (*http://nccs.urban.org*), as of 2014 there were 1,536,084 tax-exempt organizations registered in the United States, including:

♦ 961,718 public charities

♦ 96,604 private foundations

♦ 477,762 other types of nonprofit organizations, including chambers of commerce, fraternal organizations, and civic leagues

The Urban Institute's *Nonprofit Sector in Brief* publication summarizes and expands on *The Nonprofit Almanac 2012*. Learn more online at *urban.org*. Both publications highlight the growth in the number and finances of 501(c)(3) public charities, as well as key findings on private charitable contributions and volunteering, from 2000 to 2010. It's especially interesting to look at the trends from 2008 through 2010 to see the impact the recession had on the nonprofit sector.

To Infinity, and Beyond!
(With Apologies to Buzz Lightyear)

The top one thousand foundations in 2011 dispersed $24 billion in grants. If each dollar equaled a mile, that's the equivalent of four light years—the distance of Alpha Centauri. However, distant stars are not known grantmaking entities...yet.

food for thought

Who is Eligible?

An organization must meet certain criteria to be granted tax-exempt status under Section 501(c)(3) of the Internal Revenue Code. It must be organized and operated solely for exempt purposes, and none of its earnings may be paid to any private shareholder or individual directly or as dividends. Additionally, an organization may not be a political action or political organization, meaning that it may not attempt to influence legislation as a core component of its activities and it may not participate in any campaign activity for or against political candidates. In other words, no campaigning for individuals or lobbying public officials.

Charitable organizations cannot be organized or operated for the benefit of private interests. None of the net earnings of these organizations can benefit private shareholders or individuals, either. A nonprofit organization must put any revenue back into the organization.

Contrary to what many people think, being a nonprofit is not a mode of operating a business. It's a tax-status designation. An excise tax—think of it as a penalty—can be imposed if an organization is found to directly benefit individuals in a way we generally think of in private, for-profit companies. More importantly, an organization can lose its tax-exempt status if it's found to be in violation of the Internal Revenue Code and Regulations. In other words, 501(c)(3) nonprofit organizations exist to benefit the community, not individuals.

Foundations: The Animals in the Zoo

The problem with the term "foundation" is that it's so inexact and vague. So, let's see if we can get a handle on it.

From a grant professional's point of view (that's us!), the world of 501(c)(3) organizations is divided into two types: those that make grants, and those that don't. So, since we're in the business of grant seeking, we can ignore the ones that don't, right? Right. (Except those that *don't* often make great clients if you are a consultant!)

Let's agree that those that do make grants are foundations, and those that don't, aren't. Simple.

So far, so good. But to get a little more precise, and to follow the lead of the Council on Foundations, let's agree that, to be a foundation, it must support charitable activities of unrelated organizations or to individuals pursuing scientific, educational, cultural, religious, or other charitable purposes.

If we stop here, we'd be in good shape in understanding the concept of "foundation." That said, some folks like to complicate things by focusing on where grantmaking foundations get their funding, which is the whole "public charity" versus "private foundation" thing. In our view, this is a bit of a red herring, leading to lots of misunderstanding. But you're going to encounter it (probably already have, right?), so let's quickly discuss it, and move on to more interesting stuff.

Some grantmaking foundations get (or got) most or all of their funding from one or at least very few sources, rather from lots of donations from the public. If this brings to mind a foundation set up by a wealthy philanthropist or family, you're exactly right. Such a foundation is classified under the Internal Revenue Code as a private foundation.

So what about a foundation that receives its support from a big swath of the public rather than from just some rich dude or dudette? Yep—it's classified as a public charity.

Another way to be a public charity is to have a legal relationship to a public charity, making it a "supporting organization."

Why do we as grant professionals care where a foundation receives its funding? One answer is that it's easier to learn a foundation's giving history if it's classified as a private foundation, because a private foundation must disclose all grantees and grant amounts in its annual IRS Form 990-PF. A foundation classified as a public charity can disclose, or not disclose, this kind of information via its 990, its website, and so on.

Want to learn more? The Council on Foundations, *cof.org,* is a credible source for information on public policy related to foundations. Its website includes public policy information about charitable deductions, donor-advised funds, IRA charitable rollovers, public-philanthropic partnerships, and tax reform.

So, that's about it. Oh, for fun, if you want to impress your friends at a cocktail party, lay this one on them: a foundation classified as a private foundation has to grant, for charitable purposes, 5 percent of its assets each year. A foundation classified as a public charity does not. Now you can be the life of the party!

Corporate Foundations

Many corporations such as Google donate products, employee volunteer time, and marketing funds for the betterment of the communities in which they operate. Some corporations have separate 501(c)(3) entities to manage corporate giving.

Corporate Philanthropy: What's in a Name?

By the way, when we say "corporate" philanthropy we're using that term generically. While the entity could actually be a corporation, it could *also* be operating in another form, such as a limited liability company. So, technically, we should call it something like, "for-profit-entity philanthropy." But that just doesn't roll off the tongue like "corporate philanthropy," does it?

Here's another bit of trivia: a corporate "foundation" might not actually be a separate legal entity at all. It might just be a program operated under the roof of the for-profit entity. This is quite common, actually. Or, it might actually be a separate legal entiity, typically receiving its funding from the for-profit entity. In that case, it's most likely classified as a private foundation—which you already figured out from the discussion above, right?

observation

Corporate philanthropy refers to the investments and activities a company voluntarily undertakes to responsibly manage its impact on society or to make a difference in the community that supports its business. This includes investments of money, donations of products, in-kind services and technical assistance, employee volunteerism, and other business transactions to advance a social cause, issue, or the work of a nonprofit organization. Corporate foundations and corporate giving programs traditionally play a major role in these areas.

Locating Funding Sources

The methods you can use to locate funding sources are as varied as the number of grant experts. The most common method is to use a search engine such as Google or Bing. This method may be very labor-intensive and relies on keyword search algorithms that those platforms use. However, this is a free source (if you're not counting your time as money spent).

Another way to find funding sources is to use a funder search service such as Grant Station or Foundation Search. These are searchable services that can find foundations based on keyword searches or other specific criteria such as geographic location, types of projects funded, or awards granted by a specific foundation. Of course, all of this information is available for free. What you pay for with these services is for the research to be done for you. These search services charge a subscription fee which can be a monthly or annual fee. You'll want to fully research these search services before spending your (or your organization's) money.

A third way to find private funding sources is search on your own with free services such as the Foundation Center and GuideStar. These two platforms offer free and paid search versions. However, you can access the Foundation Center for free by using one of its cooperative collections found at major community library branches or through university libraries. Only you (or your organization) can decide how much time and money you can devote to prospect research.

The final way to search for private foundations is to conduct the research yourself by looking up foundation websites and by poring through the foundation's IRS Form 990s. Form 990 is a tax reporting form like the tax form 1040 people use to file their federal taxes. A foundation's Form 990 lists its assets, how much it earns on investments, how its money is invested, board members or officers, who it awarded grants to in the past year, how much it awarded, and the instructions on how to apply and who to contact. If the foundation doesn't accept unsolicited proposals, it must be stated on the Form 990 as well.

Learning about Specific Funders

Learning about specific funders is both useful and necessary, especially when well-meaning colleagues and friends toss you the names of funders like rocket-propelled ping-pong balls. Grant funder "advice" from the uninitiated can be frustrating. Be prepared to positively and succinctly nip it in the bud with a few well-placed facts of your own. For example, the largest shipping provider in the world does not accept unsolicited grant proposals, despite making about $41 million in grants each year. That usually keeps them quiet for a week or so!

The best ways for you to learn about specific funders include researching at the library, researching online, reading annual reports, reviewing 990 forms, calling program officers, and making inquiries via your professional networks (such as online listserves).

Unsolicited grant proposals are grant applications that are not specifically requested by the funding source. This is like submitting your resume to a potential employer without responding to a job posting or announcement. Expect similar results with this grant-seeking technique.

A funder usually publishes grant application materials and a deadline for submissions on its website. If the funder doesn't have a website, you'll need to call the program officer or seek additional information from the funder's 990s through paid or free online grant research databases. Very small foundations often do not have their own websites.

> ### Funding Source
>
> A *funding source* is the entity providing the funds. A funder is also known as the grantmaker, the donor, or the grantor.
>
>

Maintaining and Tracking Funder Information

Whether you do your prospect research in-house, or turn it over to an external consulting firm, you'll end up with a lot of information to keep track of. In-house prospecting may be faster, especially in managing communication and internal approval processes. But external research firms may be able to give you more expertise and background research on potential donors.

If you're working with an external consultant, make sure to clarify who "owns" the information the consultant provides to your organization. Once a prospect becomes a donor, your organization must acknowledge and protect donor privacy. Any grant consultant should be working closely with your organization all along to make sure you're seeking funds strategically. Strategic grant seeking is discussed further in **Chapter Three** of this manual.

You can, and should, keep track of potential funders by keeping your own log, notebook, or spreadsheet, or maintaining this information in your organization's customer relations management (CRM) system. By the way, this can also be called, simply, donor software.

Maintaining clear, concise research records in a database, in files, via a spreadsheet, or in the Cloud is crucial to successful grant seeking. When you leave your employer, it must be able to continue on with timely submission of reports, responding to funders, and grant seeking without having to start from scratch. Of course, the information ethically and legally belongs to the organization, not you.

There are probably as many ways to track grant funders as there are professionals who track them. Most professionals we know use either donor databases or spreadsheets. Whatever system you choose should be useful to the organization you work with. Many of these systems track the foundation or funder name, amount requested, amount awarded, timeline for use of the funds, when reports are due, and who is responsible for the reports and for ensuring the deliverables are met. You may also want to track grant cycle dates, funder areas of interest, and contact information. We also advise you to keep a log of foundations that are not good prospects—not on every one, but on those foundations recommended by friends, coworkers, and board members. Then you'll have a quick answer when someone says, "Let's apply to the *XYZ Foundation*. It funded my brother-in-law's organization." Never mind that the two organizations serve completely different target populations!

Organization's Impact on Grant Seeking

The world's most meticulous grant research won't amount to a hill of beans if the organization seeking grant funding doesn't have the infrastructure, skills, and leadership to effectively manage grant funds and report on outcomes. Without disparaging beans, another way to state this is that an organization must be "grant-ready" to effectively pursue and manage potential funding.

How do you know if an organization is grant ready? In some cases, this is a subjective analysis. An organization's personnel, finances, and other resources that affect grant readiness can change rapidly. To be grant ready, an organization should minimally have an operating budget; a functioning board of directors; a current strategic plan; a history of receiving and spending funds in a timely, legal manner; and cash reserves in case of operational emergencies.

Grant-ready

Grant-ready describes an organization's capacity to seek and manage grant funds, implement projects, and close out grant funding.

Of course, having a good strategic plan and a sound budget aren't the only items your organization needs to apply for and manage grant funds. You need to look closely at your culture, mission, and organizational values. Does your organization strive for excellence, or do you accept mediocrity? Do you easily identify a project manager and hold that person accountable for implementation, or do you assign a program to a department and hope or assume it will get done? These important questions (and many more) are some of the things you'll need to think about when deciding to seek grant funds. If you can't properly manage the funds, don't apply. Think of it as your money. We bet you'll look at the issue a little more clearly now!

Identifying Fundable Programs and Projects

To be fundable, a program or project must address a certain geographic or target community. It must also meet a need or focus area that the funder has identified. For example, a mobile food pantry based at a local food bank is fundable. So is an organization that's increasing access to quality food in an underserved community. On the other hand, providing free water and healthy snack stations for well-heeled but exhausted shoppers at an upscale shopping area is probably not fundable, at least not by foundations. Hydration is important, but if shoppers can afford designer heels, they can spring for their own water and edamame. Funders want to address community needs, not individual desires. If you were a funder, would you want to give your money to the people in the mall, or to an organization providing food in poverty-stricken areas? Of course, there are funders that provide grants to individuals, mostly in the form of scholarships.

Dry-mouthed power shoppers aside, let's consider the two basic elements of being fundable. One is to be eligible based on demonstrated need and the target community to be served. The second element is whether the proposed program or project is well-designed and could be replicated in other settings. Innovation is also an important element of fundable grant projects. Consider the mobile food pantry, for example. It serves the hungry and is well-designed to transport and distribute a lot of food, fast. But the innovation could be partnering with a local school that has a health clinic to help families access several basic services at once.

You'll also need to consider the idea of a project or program. Most funders and foundations are attracted to projects because it allows them to hang their hat on a concept that has a beginning and an end. Indefinite time limits and ongoing projects are often less interesting to funders. General operating support is one of these ideas. All organizations need general operating support, but few granting agencies like to make these types of awards. Other ongoing costs that help fill the gap between program cost and what consumers can afford to pay, such as day care program fees or healthcare costs for low-income clients, may not be fundable, either. The gap is real, but grant funding to bridge the gap is often not available. Other forms of fundraising such as major donors, annual appeals, and special events can help cover these costs. These forms of fundraising are covered in other CharityChannel Press In the Trenches titles.

> ### Fundable
>
> *Fundable* is the likelihood that a project or concept is attractive to funders and grantmakers.
>
>

Determining Best Matches

The best funder and program matches are the ones that assist both in achieving their missions.

The best way to play matchmaker as a grant professional is to align a funder's goals with a specific, well-designed project with reportable outcomes. The mission, vision, and goals of the funder must be in sync with your organization's mission, vision, and goals—or at least they should complement one another.

You must do your homework here to begin the process. We've heard from many foundation program officers that they detest calls from grant-seekers asking what types of projects the foundation supports or what their deadlines are, when the information is clearly stated on their website. The grant professional must do this basic research to see if the foundation is interested in the same issues and causes as the organization seeking funds. You wouldn't apply for a line cook position at a bank (unless it had its own kitchen). Similarly, you cannot expect a foundation that supports children's causes to fund your program that serves animals or the elderly. A little bit of time spent conducting some basic research will pay off later in better relationships with foundation officers. Remember, we all run in professional circles. You don't want to get a poor reputation among funders.

Another Type of Match

You may also hear people refer to "matching funds" in another way, whereby the donor agrees to match dollar-for-dollar, or some other ratio, any funds raised.

Local match is another common term in the grant profession. Many federal government grants, for example, require at a minimum a 20 percent local match, with the grant funds contributing 80 percent of the total project costs. The grantee may be required to cover additional costs over and above the 20 percent requirement, often referred to as *over-match*.

In philanthropic giving, foundations and corporations often give money to nonprofit entities in the form of matching gifts. Corporate matches often take the form of employee matching gifts. In other words, if an employee donates to a nonprofit, the employee's company will donate money to the same nonprofit according to a predetermined match ratio (usually 1:1) up to a set amount.

For foundations, matching gifts are in the form of grants made directly to nonprofits under the qualifying condition that the nonprofit raise a set amount of money before the grant is awarded. These grants are great because they give you greater leverage when you're fundraising from your constituency. If a foundation approves a 1:1 matching grant, donors know their dollars will be doubled. At the same time, foundations that give matching grants are assured of your organization's capacity to raise adequate funds.

Interpreting Funder Intent

Funder intent can be a tricky thing to assess. The grant application or RFP is a good place to start. However, the RFP is usually designed to elicit a response from potential grantees rather than for the funder to share the intent of the funds.

The RFP is a wealth of information for the grant seeker. Everything you need to know about completing a potentially successful application or proposal is in the RFP. We suggest you read the RFP once over to get a general idea of what the funder is asking for and then read it again for detail. Jot down notes, underline or highlight, or use tags or other colorful noting devices such as Sticky Notes to draw attention to specific information. The RFP will usually specify who's eligible to apply, due dates, formatting requirements for the proposal, and the funder's stated goals and objectives.

RFP

An RFP is a request for proposals. This is the document used by funders to describe the specific requirements of a successful proposal.

If you read the RFP and you're trying to make your project fit the guidelines, you're probably not going to be successful. When matched appropriately, the RFP will ask for much of what you have to offer in your project. The match should be mostly seamless, although a few bumps or misalignments may happen. You can't fit a square peg into a round hole.

Government Grantmakers

If you want to assess funder intent for government grantmakers, you should start by reading the authorizing legislation. The legislation, budget information, or continuing authorization will be spelled out and cited in the RFP or grant application, which is sometimes called a Request for Applications (RFA) by public or government entities.

If the grant program has been around a few years, the funder's intent is detailed on the grantor agency's website. The next place you can look is on the agency's website, which lists past grantees. Grantmaking agencies may be required to share the results of their grantmaking activities, and their report to Congress may be posted on the agency's website. Another way to gauge funder intent is to ask! The agency's program officer is a terrific source of information. Government grantmakers also host grant application workshops. Attendance in some cases is mandatory, but even voluntary attendance may prove valuable to you in determining funder intent.

Private Grantmakers

The best way to start assessing a private grantmaker's intent is to look at its annual reports. The annual reports are important for a couple of reasons:

◆ Evaluating to whom, for what, and the dollar amount of their past giving can shed light on the funder's intent.

◆ The annual reports may provide a look back at giving levels and toward the future expectations for grantees.

Additionally, review the annual report for grantees and recipients in your local marketplace. You or someone on your board of directors may have a personal connection with a past recipient. You could partner with that organization on another grant or interview the program staff in regard to the award process, including project management and outcome measurements. Grantmakers provide a lot of information on their website about their spending and giving programs.

The IRS requires all nonprofits and charities to register and obtain an Employer Identification Number (EIN) or Tax Identification Number (TIN). The EIN/TIN is similar to an individual's Social Security number. Grantmakers, nonprofits, and charities that are classified as private foundations (which we discuss above) must file a tax-exempt status form called a IRS Form 990-PF. The PF stands for private foundation. The 990-PF forms are public records and can be found online. Many foundations publish their 990s on their websites. The 990 form contains information about the organization's financials, grants, charitable giving, paid staff, volunteers, and board of directors. You can use this document to evaluate funder intent and determine who the decision makers are at the grantmaking organization.

Are You Exam Ready?

You are exam ready if you can:

◆ Identify major trends in public funding and public policy

◆ Identify major trends in private grant funding

◆ Identify methods of locating funding sources

◆ Identify techniques to learn about specific funders

◆ Identify methods for maintaining, tracking, and updating information on potential funders

◆ Identify effects of applicants' organizational cultures, values, decision making processes, and norms on the pursuit of grant opportunities

◆ Identify fundable programs and projects for specific organizations

◆ Determine best matches between funders and specific programs

◆ Identify and interpret grant application RFP guidelines and requirements to accurately assess funder intent

Chapter Two

Organizational Development

IN THIS CHAPTER

···➔ How do I know if my organization is grant ready?

···➔ Does organizational structure affect our ability to seek grants?

···➔ How does an organization become grant ready?

···➔ When does organizational planning impact grants?

Before crafting that first paragraph, make sure your organization is "grant ready," that is, able to qualify for, seek, and manage grants. Many nonprofit organization leaders and board members assume that, since they are a designated 501(c)(3) by the IRS, they're automatically able to receive grant funding. That's like assuming that you can be a champion marathoner just because you have a pair of running shoes. Yes, anyone can write proposals, but it takes a lot more to show that your organization is worthy of receiving grant funding.

What is organization development? One classic definition comes from Richard Beckhard's 1969 book, *Organization Development: Strategies and Models*:

> *Organization Development is an effort (1) planned, (2) organization-wide, and (3) managed from the top, to (4) increase organization effectiveness and health through (5) planned interventions in the organizations "processes," using behavioral science knowledge.*

A more current definition comes from Matt Minahan from MM & Associates in Silver Spring, Maryland:

> *Organization Development is a body of knowledge and practice that enhances organizational performance and individual development, by increasing alignment among the various systems within the overall system. OD interventions are inclusive methodologies and approaches to strategic planning, organization design, leadership development, change management, performance management, coaching, diversity, team building, and work/life balance.*

So, organization development goes beyond crafting the ideal grant or putting together the perfect project development team. Sound organizational development is crucial to a well-run, effective organization. A well-run, effective organization is likely to get more grants!

Organizational Capacity to Seek Grant Funding

The first step in becoming grant ready is to assess your organizational capacity to handle the funds if the proposals are funded. All funders, whether they are individual donors or grantmaking organizations, are essentially investors in your programs and services. Look at the process as if you were the investor being asked to support this organization. What would you look for? What questions would you ask of its leaders?

Another important step in grant readiness is assessing how an organization accepts and manages funds. In other words, what processes are in place to account for and manage this money? A good place to start is with the accounting department.

There are three types of accounting practices: cash, accrual, and a combination of the two. Small organizations may be able to work on a cash accounting system, but most organizations use an accrual system. The difference between cash and accrual accounting is when the revenue and expenses are recognized and accounted for. If your organization recognizes revenue when it receives a check or payment for services, then it's using a cash accounting system. If your organization recognizes revenue when it invoices someone after a service has been provided, then it operates on an accrual system. There are advantages and disadvantages to both systems, and the details are beyond the scope of this manual. Knowing how your organization handles its accounting helps with fund management. Larger funders will ask you about the type of system your organization (or client) uses.

Cash versus Accrual Accounting

Cash accounting is based on recognizing the revenue when the organization receives payment for a service or product. *Accrual accounting* recognizes revenue when it is earned. Similarly, cash accounting recognizes the expenditures when the service or product is purchased, whereas accrual accounting recognizes the expense when it is paid.

Hopefully, no one at your organization is keeping cash donations under a mattress or producing budgets using crayons and Monopoly money. Once the accounting system is sorted out, take a look at other key issues. How are the funds separated and accounted for? Public and government funders will expect you to have separate accounts for their grant funds. This doesn't mean you need a separate bank account. But a specific fund code must be in place for each specific restricted grant to make sure expenses are properly tracked and accounted for.

No one wants to be the hapless grant writer who's hauled into court because the federal grant funds ended up in a shady condo deal on a desert island. Unfortunately, there are too many instances when the person who wrote the grant winds up in court over the crimes that someone else committed. To be a successful grant professional, you need to fully understand the basic financial practices of your organization. The questions you need to ask include:

◆ How are expenses tracked?

◆ What's expected of employees when funds are spent?

◆ Does your organization have a financial audit on a regular basis? Having a financial audit is an important way to prove to others that your organization follows nationally approved guidelines called generally accepted accounting principles, or GAAPs. Most organizations have an audit conducted by an outside firm once per year, but sometimes smaller organizations are audited every two years.

> ## Generally Accepted Accounting Principles
>
> GAAP standards are a nationally-recognized set of accounting standards that all individuals who work in finance fields are expected to follow.
>
> definition

Some states don't require audits, while others require them if the organization meets a minimum threshold of revenue, or if it meets certain thresholds with regard to solicitation of charitable contributions. You should make certain that you are familiar with the state-mandated audit requirements for the organization.

The federal government can also require a "single audit" report if your organization spends $750,000 or more in federal contract dollars in any given fiscal year. This is often called an OMB A-133 audit.

It should be noted that financial audits should be conducted by an outside firm, and not one that provides ongoing accounting services to your organization.

Additionally, your organization's board of directors should vote on the outside firm it uses each year. Senior leaders should choose a different firm every few years, unless the current accounting firm changes the accounting professionals who perform the audit every few years. This practice helps ensure that errors are uncovered and that collusion and impropriety are not taking place.

Most grant applications require a fairly standard set of financial documents. These documents give the funder a picture of the financial health of your organization. Common documents are balance sheets and income statements.

Balance sheets list the various types of assets and liabilities your organization owns. A balance sheet lists assets in terms of liquidity and liabilities in terms of payables due. Someone looking at a balance sheet will be able to quickly tell how rapidly you can pay your bills and what you own that could be sold in times of great need. They can also see the types of debt you have and whether those debts are short or long term.

Income statements are sometimes called profit and loss or P&L statements. This document demonstrates your agency's current picture against budget and in terms of income and expenditures. Ideally, your organization is bringing in more money than it spends. An income statement also compares your current or year-end statement against the proposed budget. This tells a funder how well your organization forecasts revenue and expenses and how well program staff and leaders follow their budgets. In the right hands, these documents are like an MRI for your organization. Savvy funders can diagnose the overall financial health of your organization with them.

Grant readiness isn't all about the numbers. Several other key documents make up the list of most commonly requested information in grant applications. Keep an archive of your mission statement, values statement, tax-status determination letter, current board roster, agency goals and year-to-date status of progress, organizational chart, and description of current programs. Maintaining files of these routinely requested documents will save you hours in preparing grant proposals. An organization that doesn't have or can't produce these basic documents is definitely not grant ready.

Keep in mind that different funders may require slight variations on the basic documents. For example, some funders want a list of names of board members, while others require much more detail. A master list of board member information, updated at the start of each fiscal year, can streamline grant preparation. Associations are important to funders so they can see what skills your board members bring and determine if there are any possible conflicts of interest with their foundation officers.

Some funders will also want to ensure your board is reflective of the clientele your organization serves. Whenever possible, having clients on your board, or serving in an advisory capacity, is a good idea. If you serve infants or rescued animals, board service would not, of course, be a good idea. It would be a great photo opportunity, though. Seriously, having clients serve in an appropriate capacity ensures that your organization receives the most current information, ideas, and suggestions to keep improving.

Gender, racial, and ethnic identification are required by some funders. Even if it is not required, this demographic data can enhance a proposal if your board members are diverse on many levels and if they are representative of the clientele you serve. Ideally, your board list tells a story about the experience and backgrounds of those who fundraise and advise the operations of your organization. Being able to share that information in an attachment saves room in your proposal for other key details—a must in space-limited proposals.

Do You Have a File on... *All of Your Board Members?*

You should keep a master list with several pieces of information about each board member, so you can quickly compile the board list components that the funder requests. Your board list should include the following: name, board position (if applicable), address, email, phone number, associations, employers, gender identification, racial and ethnic identification, and age.

food for thought

Organizational Structure

Good leadership and a solid management structure are important in grant seeking to ensure program success and good stewardship of the funds. For a funder, an organizational chart can help determine how the well the organization functions and manages funds. The size of an organization does, of course, determine a lot about its organizational structure.

A midsized organization typically has departments and a leadership team. Department directors, vice presidents, or other employees with similar titles form the leadership team. They're responsible for making sure that their respective areas operate efficiently, meet performance goals, and stay within budget.

Most organizations have a chief financial officer (CFO) or finance director whose job it is to ensure that the organization's financial management is conducted in accordance with GAAP. The CFO may also interact with a finance committee of the board of directors. This interaction forms a needed set of checks and balances for sound fiscal management.

Funders may rarely, if ever, request documentation of this kind of detail. Make sure, however, to understand these roles and responsibilities within your organization. No one wants to give your blood, sweat, and tears to win a major grant only to see it mishandled or misappropriated. As a grant professional, you should have confidence that your finance department will spend the program grant on program-related expenses, not shore up payroll or renovate the break room.

GAAP and the American Institute of Certified Public Accountants require a separation of duties in organizations to ensure that funds, especially cash, are handled appropriately. This reduces the likelihood of fraud and theft and shows that your organization is a good steward of donor and/or public funds. The separation of duties includes having specifically identified positions and people who open mail, log cash and checks, post items to the ledger, and deposit funds into the bank. The more separation of duties, the more likely the organization will avoid a loss of funds. The financial head of the organization must continually monitor these functions and distribution of work.

In smaller organizations, most individuals are responsible for a variety of functions. The CEO or executive director may also write grant proposals and serve as the development officer. The important point to remember is that each organization is designed to function the best it can, given its size and type of services. These will often be modified over time as the organization grows and responds to the changing landscape of the community and the issues it was created to address.

Preparing for Grant Seeking

We've covered organizational structure and basic documentation. Now let's review how they work together in grant seeking. Your organization was founded to respond to a community need. While this need and focus may have changed over the years, you are still in business to fill a service gap. So, how do you know if your organization is still relevant or if you should change direction?

A community needs assessment helps your organization stay relevant to the community it serves. For example, a workforce development program could get wonderful reviews for its great instructors and friendly environment. But if it's teaching typewriter repair, it's not offering a relevant service for today's employment needs.

A needs assessment doesn't have to involve reams of paperwork and countless hours of meetings. With some structure and guidance, it can be a project that empowers your team and solidifies your position in the community. An effective needs assessment includes identification of your community, identification of your client pool, current resources for your clients, and gaps in those resources.

Suppose you run a food pantry that serves fifty low-income people a month. A good needs assessment may show that the number of people in need has tripled in the last five years, or that the nutritional needs of your clients have changed as people from different ethnicities have moved to your area. Gathering this type of data also builds a strong case for increased funding, or funding from different sources.

Let's see how an effective community needs assessment helps to prove or dispel your assumptions.

The first step is to set some boundaries around your assessment. You cannot take on the entire state, of course, so choose where you want to concentrate. For example, focus on the city or county where you operate. We know that we want to see what the food needs are in the county. The next step would be to determine what types of data you want to look at that can support your theory. In our example, we can find data that tells us the total population of our county, poverty rates, ages, unemployment rates, rates of high school graduation and college degree attainment, household sizes, single parent-led households, and rates of health insurance coverage. This data could help us draw a picture of what individuals in our community face. When we compare that data to other communities or to the state as a whole, we can draw some conclusions about why people go hungry and need to seek out our food pantry.

Data should be collected for a number of years in order to identify trends. One year will only tell us what the current state is. We need to see what has happened over time to effectively plan for our organization. Have these data points moved significantly over the past five years? We can draw some conclusions based on whether changes have happened or not.

Now that you have some basic demographics of the organization's community and the individuals in it, you should also begin to look at other information that can tell you how much your organization's services may be needed in the future. Is there work taking place to bring economic growth and jobs to

Trending Now!

Trend data is defined as three or more of a particular data set. For example, poverty rates over three to five years would be trend data, whereas rates over one or two years is not. The longer your data points cover, the more confidence you can begin to have that the current set of data isn't a fluke or one-time event.

the area in the next few years? Are there likely to be cuts in jobs or is growth projected to be stagnant? Do local employers pay a living wage? Do people have to travel long distances to get to work or does your community have viable public transportation? All of this information, and probably much more, will have an impact on the number of people who need and seek your organization's services.

What was described above is considered *secondary data*, defined as data obtained from other sources. Your needs assessment should also contain *primary data*, or that which you obtain yourself. This can be done through interviews or surveys. Certainly, getting the opinions of those you already serve is important. Hopefully you're already gathering your client data about how they perceive your services. The voice of your customers can provide you with valuable information.

The data collected and the work done to create the community needs assessment is a valuable tool for grant professionals. Citing this work and using the data contained within will demonstrate to funders that your organization has done its homework and is a credible source to deal with the issues.

You will also want to know what else your clients need and the other organizations that may be meeting those needs. You may find out that a new company is going to relocate to your county and many new jobs are expected to be available. To best meet your clients' needs, you would want to know what types of jobs will be available and what skills are needed to obtain those jobs. Suppose some of those jobs are entry level and your clients need help to be ready. Your organization may want to consider adding services to help move people to sustainable work or partnering with an organization that can provide those services. This does not mean you should be the provider, but knowing what services are available that can supplement what you offer or where there are gaps in services will help your organization plan to address the changing needs of the community.

Primary and Secondary Data

Primary data is that which you collect yourself through surveys, interviews, and focus groups. *Secondary data* is obtained through other sources such as census, health, or economic data.

Now you have identified your community, your clients, and their needs. You are prepared to seek funders to match your needs. How do you decide which funders to work with and to which funding opportunities to respond?

Grant seeking should always be part of the organization's overall development plan rather than a stand-alone function. Some needs are best met through fundraising, including major gifts, annual fund, planned giving, and events. General operating support is a good example of such a need. Most grant funders are interested in funding projects, not general operating support. Of course, there are some foundations that support general operating support, but most do not.

Once you have identified a funder that supports your type of organization or cause, the next step is deciding what program to seek funding for. Most organizations have needs in multiple program areas and decisions need to be made to maximize the request from each funder. If a foundation accepts proposals for youth programs, your organization must decide if it will apply for support of the early childhood program or the afterschool tutoring program. Most foundations will only accept one proposal per organization per cycle or year.

How do you make those decisions as an organization? Should the grant professional be the decision maker? Should the department head or CEO make that decision? The answer really depends on how your organization is set up. Generally, these decisions are best made with the leadership team with input from the grant professional.

The grant professional should identify the funding source, parameters, and due date. This information as well as some suggestions for programs that fit the funder's interests should be submitted to the leadership team so that the needs of the organization are matched with the funding opportunities. The grant professional should facilitate the discussion or provide the information needed to make this decision.

How Grants Fit into the Development Plan

Grant seeking belongs with the development or fund-seeking team of an organization and should be coordinated with the overall funding plan. Together this team can assess fundable projects to determine the best type of revenue to seek: grants, direct mail, major gifts, special events, etc. Sometimes the best way to fund a project is through a combination of these sources. Moving from conception of an idea or the identification of a need, the development team should work closely with the organization's leadership team to determine how the need will be funded.

Organizations need to determine what works for them. Their methods may change over time. One way to address project funding is to have all department leaders meet with the development team once the budgeting process begins. The department heads bring a list of ideas, projects, and needs for the next year and this group, along with the development team, determine how these needs are best addressed. The development team can provide feedback to the leadership team about the projects that may appeal to donors versus those that may match a foundation's giving guidelines.

In a perfect world this is a seamless, peaceful process. For many grant professionals, this process is only a pipe dream. Your reality may be more of a series of program staff members plopping down in front of you and detailing their pet projects. Or, some staffers may have empowered themselves to apply for a small-scale piece of equipment from a funder you were planning to ask for a six-figure grant. For a grant professional, this is an opportunity to educate and coordinate efforts.

One way to streamline this process is to have joint meetings on a quarterly basis. This gives the development team a chance to adjust its funding plans as the organization's needs change. Also, the meetings allow the development team to formally update the leadership team on the funding landscape as it changes due to new RFPs being released, grants being awarded or denied, and donor interests changing or new donors identified.

Organizational Readiness for Funding and Projects

One of the ways in which organizations can determine if they are ready to seek, apply for, and effectively use grant funds is to look at their organizational structure. Some questions to ask are:

- ◆ Who will do the research to discover the funders who are most likely to fund a specific project?

- ◆ Who will be able to match the funder's guidelines to the organization's needs?

- ◆ Who will contact and build the relationship with the funder or program officer?

◆ Who will manage the grant activities and ensure the deliverables are met if the project is funded?

◆ Who will ensure the funds are spent properly?

◆ Who will manage the relationship with the funder during the process?

The answers to these questions will begin to lead the organization toward putting a structure in place to manage grants. Grant seeking is not simply looking for grants and applying for the funds. The work continues during the award process in answering questions from the funder or providing additional documentation if requested. The work also includes properly thanking the funder whether or not you were funded.

Winning a grant is only the beginning. Allocating expenses, tracking program performance and outcomes, and reporting on time to the funder are key aspects of grant management that often cross department lines. Poor or lax grant management is a great way to not receive funding in the future, and not just from the foundation that trusted your organization with its investment. Foundations are made of people, and they'll talk to each other about their grantees.

A seasoned grant professional will contact a funder as soon as possible to explain the situation. Waiting until the final report is overdue to reveal that your pet shelter roof is in a different county, or that it took five months instead of two to complete a training module, won't help.

Program officers have often worked in organizations similar to yours. Hearing about your struggles sooner, rather than later, will give them confidence that you're handling their investment wisely. Many times, they can provide some assistance or referrals. You can often work with them to adjust the timeline or redirect expenditures. But if you only let them in after the fact or at the end of the funding year, you've let your partner down. It affects your ability to seek funds from that foundation again, and it may affect your future funding possibilities within your community. Reputations matter.

Should You Thank All Funders?

Even Nonfunders?

Yes, you should *always* thank the funder even if you weren't awarded the funds. Someone at the foundation took the time to read your proposal (probably more than once), give it thought, and measure it against many other proposals. The foundation gave you significant time and energy and deserves your appreciation. Besides—you'll stand out in the crowd the next time you apply.

Practices That Advance Grant Readiness

So, what can your organization do to make it grant ready? There are several things your organization can do. First, you should have an organizational structure in place to make sure your operations run smoothly. Accountability across the organization tells funders that you're able to handle the many aspects of managing their funds. Checks and balances are important to making sure everything is done— on time and with fidelity. If the bills are not paid on time, reports not completed, and goals consistently not met, the organization isn't being run well. A checks and balances system must be in place so that if someone is out of the office or leaves the organization, the functions of their position are still done. When an organization lacks accountability, people notice. The organization begins to get a poor reputation in the community, which is counterproductive to seeking grants.

Secondly, an organization must have solid accounting principles. It must be able to account for and manage funds from all sources. This means that the bills are paid, customers are invoiced quickly, a system is in place to prevent fraud, bank statements are reconciled, and an external audit is conducted at least every other year. Small organizations may have a difficult time affording an audit every year, but they shouldn't go more than two years without one. This is an important step in proving to funders that the organization has appropriate practices in place and it uses its funds appropriately.

Finally, documentation is critical to successful grant seeking. Your organization should have a basic set of documents that are often asked for as attachments in many RFPs. These include your tax-status

> ### Life Happens to Grants, Too
>
> Believe or not, not all grants go as planned. Shocking, isn't it? Once in a while, life happens, and your grant project is derailed. Maybe you didn't get enough additional funds to fully implement the project. Maybe a key person left the organization and you couldn't hire a qualified replacement in time to complete the deliverables. Maybe a hurricane or tornado ripped through your facility and shut it down for weeks.
>
> **observation**

determination letter, board roster, current balance sheet, financial audit, current income statement, agency organizational chart, and a list of programs or services. Additionally, you should also have copies of your agency newsletters and annual reports in case you need to attach them to your proposal or application. They give an overview of the functioning of your organization.

Keep files on overall program outcomes and compelling individual stories as well. These pieces will tell a powerful story about how effective your organization is at meeting the needs of the community. Don't be afraid to add these pieces (if you are permitted, of course). They're great additions when applications provide a section for "additional information."

Obtaining Institutional Support for Grant-seeking Activities

If grant funding is the best way to support your project, make sure you have the appropriate approvals from senior leaders to move forward. Don't spend hours finding a potential funder and crafting a solid proposal only to find out that your CEO is not on board. Why would a CEO not want to pursue a grant? Sometimes projects do not have full institutional support or may not fully meet the mission. This can happen when individuals continually chase grant money through responding to RFPs instead of seeking partners who can fund the activities of the organization. One way to mitigate this risk is to have a grant project approval form. Then you'll have a paper trail of approval just in case.

Another advantage to obtaining institutional support for grant seeking is to engage the power of your board of directors. If you have board members who are acquainted with key individuals at the foundation or who are friends with the board members of the foundation, they can provide additional support for your proposal. This can be done purposefully, such as a board member contacting a friend on the board of the foundation, or informally, if a board member meets the foundation's board member at an event and asks about the organization or the project. It would be very awkward for your board member not to talk about a proposal, especially if you are aware of the person's connection to the foundation. If board members know about your proposals and the programs they'll fund, they'll be able to make connections to potential donors and better promote the organization.

Strategic Planning

Let's turn our attention to how grants fit into your organization's plans.

What's in a Grant Project Approval Form?

The grant project approval form should include the following:

◆ Name of the project

◆ Scope of the project

◆ Timeframe for the project

◆ Name of the funder

◆ Name of the project manager

◆ Amount to be requested, total cost of project, and other funding sources

◆ Timeline for the application process

◆ Place for signatures of key decision makers

 practical tip

Strategic planning hones an organization's focus and objectives. The process and its implications are beyond the scope of this refresher manual. However, grant seeking is also an intentional process that helps an organization meet its goals. A seasoned grant professional doesn't haphazardly dash off applications because a board member or other well-intentioned individual heard about an open request for proposals.

As your organization's leaders review its mission, vision, and strategic direction, they'll also discuss funding activities to fulfill the mission. The grants plan is part of the overall development plan, but the grant professional is critical to the discussion. This person has the knowledge of the local foundations and the federal and state application cycles and outlines. This information rounds out the development plan, which in turn helps support the activities that achieve the goals of the strategic plan.

For example, if your organization's strategic plan outlines the need to expand a tutoring program to three more schools to help students who are performing below grade level, then the funding plan will be created to identify foundations and other funding sources that can support these activities. Is there a donor who could provide seed money for the expansion or are there foundations whose guidelines include tutoring programs? Do you have a young professionals or other fundraising group that could more easily raise money to support this program? All of these activities must be coordinated and built around the strategic plan in order to achieve success.

Working with Local, State, and Federal Agencies and Stakeholders

Support for grant seeking should reach beyond the walls of your organization. Besides your board, it's important to involve other stakeholders in your community. When the schools operate well, more families move in and the community begins to flourish. When a tutoring program is successful, the students, families, and the community-at-large win because those young people become citizens who contribute to the overall well-being. When the police department has the latest equipment and training, it is more fully able to keep the community safe.

How can grant professionals involve their community leaders? Newsletters and open houses are a good way to keep everyone informed on a regular basis. Letters of support are tangible ways in which police chiefs, school superintendents, mayors, and other elected officials can show support for your application or proposal. Since you've kept them informed of your programs and accomplishments, obtaining these letters should be relatively easy. Give them plenty of lead time to allow for longer processes in larger organizations.

If you haven't kept your local officials in the loop, don't despair. Asking for a letter of support will give you a chance to update them on your organization's key accomplishments and the need for additional funding. Even if they decline to give you a letter this time, reopening the lines of communication could lead to other letters or additional support in the future.

State support is also an important area to address. While the governor or state school superintendent may not be on your contact list, you should seek these people out. Again, they have a stake in your work. Of course, politics can affect any relationship, but you'll be surprised at how many elected officials want to help. A strong community makes a stronger state. The same goes for seeking federal support. Everybody comes from a smaller community or neighborhood. These individuals care deeply about their home communities. Besides, what elected officials pass up an opportunity to show their constituents how involved they are locally? Including letters of support from local, state, and federal stakeholders will strengthen your proposal or application by demonstrating that you're involved with your community outside of your organization.

Groupthink Does It Again

Groupthink is a product of unhealthy or ineffective organizational development. First used in 1972 by social psychologist Irving L. Janis, the term refers to a psychological phenomenon in which people strive for consensus within a group. In many cases, people will set aside their own personal beliefs or adopt the opinion of the rest of the group. People who are opposed to the decisions or overriding opinion of the group as a whole frequently remain quiet, preferring to keep the peace rather than disrupt the uniformity of the crowd.

Groupthink can lead to irrational or dysfunctional decision making in the interests of conformity. It can also lead to poor grant projects. Be aware of this phenomenon and be prepared to speak out against it in the interests of better project design for grant proposals.

Grant Seeking and the Law

One of the most important things to remember in grant seeking is to always operate within the limits of the law. It's safe to assume that most grant professionals don't want to be outlaws, but ignorance can lead us in the wrong direction. GPA has a code of ethics that helps to define grey areas of operation. **Chapter Six** covers the topic more in depth. Be aware that laws can differ from state to state.

Generally, the laws and regulations that govern business practices also cover grant seeking. Paying an official for a letter of support or offering money or favors to an individual or organization to approve your proposal are "good" bad examples. More nuanced situations may call for your organization's legal counsel. The local bar association is a great place to get a referral for an attorney. Independent grant contractors and/or consultants should also identify potential legal counsel. This can be especially helpful if you run into a dispute with a client. Having trusted legal advice can give you peace of mind and may save you from a bad situation.

Are You Exam Ready?

You are exam ready if you can:

- ◆ Describe organizational development as it pertains to grant seeking

- ◆ Identify methods for coordinating organizations' grant development with various available funding streams

- ◆ Assess organizations' capacity for grant seeking

◆ Assess organizations' readiness to obtain funding for and implement specific projects

◆ Identify methods for assisting organizations to implement practices that advance grant readiness

◆ Identify values, purposes, and goals of fund-seeking entities' overall strategic plans in the grant process

◆ Identify methods of conducting mission-focused planning and needs assessments with applicant organizations

◆ Identify strategies and procedures for obtaining internal institutional support and approval of decision makers for grant-seeking activities

◆ Identify appropriate methods of working with local, state, and federal agencies and stakeholders to support grant seeking

◆ Identify practices of grant seeking that are outside the boundaries of applicable laws and regulations

Chapter Three

Good Project Design

IN THIS CHAPTER

--→ Building effective partnerships and design teams

--→ Defining a logic model

--→ Creating strong evaluation plans

--→ Planning strong sustainability in project plans

If your idea of great house is a castle on the sand or a house of cards, then good solid program design may be a challenging concept. On the other hand, if you think choosing a home with a firm foundation, solid walls, and a sound roof is a very good thing, then effective program design will be a cinch. Just like major home construction projects, building sound program design takes about twice as long as you think and can involve lots of meetings.

Consider this chapter our version of HGTV for project plans and program design, without the fancy TV production values and infomercials. Basically, we'll be looking at effective program design and offering tips for creating collaborations that work. We believe that staying true to the process yields a well-constructed program with lots of curb appeal for funders. (Sorry about that last one.)

So, don your virtual hard hat and let's continue with this home construction analogy. For most of us, buying or building a home occurs after we qualify for a mortgage, win the lottery, or receive a legacy from a long lost relative. There's the arduous search process, and the cold, hard truth that we can't have a dream home on a nightmarishly small budget. Unless you're a real estate zillionaire, you don't start building your dream house and hope you find funding. Banks are kind of funny about that!

The same basic concepts apply to project design and the grant development process. We usually write a grant proposal because a program or project needs funding. It's pretty straightforward matchmaking. But sometimes an RFP fuels the project design. This most likely involves a program director, CEO, or board member firing off an email insisting that the organization go for a particular grant that will fund a type of program that doesn't exist at the nonprofit. Try and think of this as something like a starry-eyed real estate developer carving timeshare condos out of an abandoned cornfield because it's a flat piece of land, even though the coast or mountain range may be more than ten hours away. To be fair, cornfields can be beautiful, and some wonderful programs have started from scratch through an RFP process. But most of the time, building a program "on spec" hoping for a large grant leads to ineffective designs and frazzled grant professionals. Start early in working with your program managers to identify a clear project design outline using the logic model.

Project Design Team

When designing a new project or program, an ideal team would include the grant professional, project director, at least one direct staff member, someone from the finance team, and someone who is strong in program evaluation. If you work with a smaller organization you may have a team of two, but you really need the team to cover each of these roles to create an effective plan. Let's take a look at each role.

> ### Great Idea, Right?
>
> A colleague of ours combats the latest "great idea" from program coworkers by asking them to fill out a form she calls "Twenty Questions." This form requires the program managers to think through their ideas in a formative manner. Everything from how many people the project will serve to the sustainability plan is addressed in this document. It serves as the backbone of the project, much like the logic model does. Many grant professionals have a tool like this. We encourage you to use these tools as you begin the process.
>
> **observation**

In many organizations, the grant writer and the project director are the same person. Heck, for many of us that's just the tip of the job responsibility iceberg. So let's talk about each role separately.

The grant professional is the team member who directs the planning meetings. This person has the familiarity and relationship with the funding organization and the details of the RFP. As the grant professional in residence, you'll help discern which ideas are sound and which would put the application or proposal in jeopardy. It's part of your job to have a keen understanding of what appeals to the funder. You have this *magical* power from, at the very least, having attending the bidder's meeting or technical assistance call. At the very best, you have a strong working relationship with the funder. Remember, with great power comes great responsibility! Use your power only for good! May the force be with you! (You get the picture, right?)

The project director is the person who is most familiar with how the key elements of the project fit together with other programs. This person also understands how the project melds with the agency's strategic plan and overall goals. Project directors bring their expertise and understanding of why the project is good for the community and agency. They understand the staffing, space, client, and regulatory requirements. Project directors also know about licensed staff members or client-to-staff ratios and other programmatic requirements.

A direct staff person on the design team can provide essential front line information and a "reality check" for project design. There's little worse than winning a grant only to discover that the promised deliverables are impossible to obtain. The direct staff person has the best knowledge of what clients are likely to do or tolerate. For example, a registration form may not be appropriate or feasible for certain clients, forming an unintended barrier. The direct-service staff person can identify such potential obstacles in the project's early planning stages and may be able to offer creative solutions.

You'll need to include someone from the finance team early on so you can accurately develop the project budget and report on the budget expenditures during the project period. Very often, projects include staff salaries and fringe benefits. Having the finance department's input often saves time and creates a more realistic budget, resulting in fewer budget revisions later.

Finally, a project evaluator should be involved in the beginning of the design process. No matter how large or small your organization, identifying someone who can address the evaluation portion of the project will pay off in spades down the road. Many funders are more sophisticated about project evaluation and outcome measurement than they were ten or twenty years ago. It used to be that a "numbers served" or what we like to call a "fast food approach" to evaluation was okay and somewhat satisfying, kind of like a late night drive-through dining experience. But serving a certain number of clients or having a high percentage of clients loving what you do isn't good enough anymore. An evaluator on your project team will push the other members to think about how to determine if the project is truly making an impact.

> ## Program Staff are Vital to Program Design
>
> One of us worked in a program whereby an administrator who was not connected to the program wrote a grant proposal for us. We were awarded the funding and then learned about the deliverables. As part of the deliverables, we were required to collect and analyze data that hadn't been collected before and would have been very hard to get.
>
> A large programmatic barrier was erected because the program team members weren't consulted in the planning and writing phases. We had to make many adjustments to the program in order to meet project and funder requirements. Simply dealing with this in the beginning would have allowed us to negotiate a plan up front. The person writing the proposal was only trying to appeal to the funder with a good evaluation plan. But it ended up to be a large burden on the program staff and clients.
>
>  stories from the real world

Let's say that a perfect project design team is sitting around the conference table. What's the best way to work together? As a grant professional, you would be the obvious choice for team leader, since you're most likely coordinating the entire proposal process. Also, as a grant professional, you're awesome, and you *should* be in charge! Seriously, though, you've got this.

Before the first meeting, the team leader should provide everyone with the general scope of the project and what each member's role will be. This allows everyone to come prepared with ideas or research. During the meeting, each person should have the chance to contribute information, expertise, and creativity. Skilled diplomacy is one of the unsung talents of grant professionals! Use a logic model or other project design tool to drive the meeting agenda.

The voice of the client or customer is a critical piece, but that voice is often missing part of the project design. Too often program designers and well-meaning staff assume they know what's best for the client. Why not ask the people your team is trying to serve what they need to succeed? You might learn something.

Include clients and customers in focus groups, client interviews, or surveys. You'd be amazed at how often our customers have sound ideas on how to overcome roadblocks. Sometimes, what we think are wonderful ideas aren't so great in their eyes.

Building Partnerships

More and more organizations are working together for the common good. For bigger projects it's the best way to make larger-scale positive changes in a community. Collaboration resonates with funders. Collaboration is also a word that can strike terror in the grant professional on a deadline.

What's the best way to work together toward a common goal?

True collaboration is challenging, at best. But having a clear plan of action makes the whole process less painful for everyone involved. Start with a clear definition of the community problem. This most important factor often gets overlooked as organizations try to fill their own needs first. This is not to say we all don't have our priorities in line. It simply means that we often revert back to "what's in it for me."

Next, identify other partners that address the needs in ways that your organization can't. Don't be afraid to get creative here! A food pantry and a tutoring program may be a very good match if the students in the target population are living in poverty and if food security is a barrier to learning.

Collaboration

Collaboration is when two or more organizations join forces to help solve a community problem by bringing their specific expertise and resources together.

Think globally about the problem you're trying to address and brainstorm a list of all of the needs your clients will have. This list will help you identify potential partner organizations.

For example, suppose a community problem is individual lack of awareness with regard to HIV status. If people don't know if they have the HIV virus or not, then they could become a health threat to others in their community, specifically their sex partners. What constitutes the problem? Why don't individuals know their status? Why aren't they getting tested? Is testing not available or is it fraught with barriers? Once individuals are tested, do they know what to do? Is medical treatment available to them if they test positive? Does health insurance play a factor? Who helps these people navigate the medical system? How do they appropriately disclose their HIV status to their family, friends, and future partners? What other social issues confront a newly diagnosed individual?

This short list illustrates the many avenues a project can take. Should this project simply focus on testing or should it include other areas a person may face when interacting with this project? The project design team needs to grapple with these questions in order to build the project outline and create a partner list.

Now let's suppose we decided to provide HIV testing and help those who test positive become connected to treatment. Who else should we involve? Assuming we're the organization that can provide the testing, we need others who can provide treatment. If we're not the local health department, we may need to get it involved to provide other testing and/or partner notification services (as is required). Will these clients need a navigator or patient assistant to help them make and keep their first few appointments? Will they need help with obtaining health insurance or Medicaid? Do they have other issues such as housing, food, or employment? Will they need mental health services to work through the shock of such a diagnosis or the feelings of others in their families?

All of these questions lead us to potential collaborative partners. In the list of questions, we can see the need for a local health department, social service organization, health insurance assistance organization, public housing, food assistance, employment assistance, and mental health providers. This large team can truly effect change in a community. Here's the billion-dollar question. How do we all work together?

This concept takes us right back to the house-hunting analogy that started off this chapter. One-half of a couple wants a waterfront, open plan, and quiet retreat with a pool, hot tub, and natural stone pizza oven. The other wants an underground wine cellar in a glitzy beach house complete with a helipad. But their budget is more likely to fund a studio apartment with a pizza delivery place across the street from the beach. Unless their best friend is a popular renovation show host, compromise is job one on the house-hunting search.

Assuming your collaborative project is not likely to be funded at the full level of what every organization needs, everyone who participates in your project should be willing to bring something to give and have something they want to get. Most of these organizations are already funded from other sources, so pooling these resources is critical.

For example, the housing organization can use its funding to get the new clients into appropriate housing. Maybe it also provides classes on household budgeting so clients can remain in their homes and eventually work themselves off of housing assistance. This organization brings its programs and funding streams to the project, and it gets additional clients as well as new connections from other partners for its current clients. Partnerships can result in win-win scenarios for clients.

Funders recognize this, and organizations are sharing resources and working together creatively more than ever before. In fact, many funders are strongly suggesting that collaboration form a central part of a program or project, especially those on a larger scale.

Financial and Programmatic Accountability

In your role as a grant professional, you should know a lot about the funder and about the specific requirements of the proposal. Those outside the grant profession may think of us as silent, caffeine-fueled beings hunched over a computer screen frantically typing against deadline. Okay, sometimes that *is* an accurate picture.

But all too often we're our own worst enemies when it comes to taking on leadership roles with accountability in program design. It really is the responsibility of the grant professional to educate project team members about what processes and procedures should be in place as the organization applies for and manages any grant award. Don't be afraid to step up and explain key reporting requirements, deadlines, and financial obligations associated with the potential grant award. And don't assume that even senior level team members understand exactly how grants work. Calmly and professionally detailing the requirements may not be a glamorous role, but it's a vital one. Remember, we're grant

Memorandum of Understanding

As partnerships develop, it's good practice to have each organization sign a memorandum of understanding (MOU) or memorandum of agreement (MOA). These documents spell out what each organization brings to the collaboration and what they can expect to get. This is an important step whether or not any funds change hands. As with any agreement, it defines the dates, parameters, and protections of all parties. Client data will need to be shared in the evaluation and the MOU or MOA will address what information will be shared, with whom, and how it will be used.

Items for the MOU should include:

◆ Legal name and address of each organization

◆ Name of the project

◆ Expectations of each organization with due dates

◆ Beginning and end dates

◆ Termination clause

◆ Signatures from authorized representatives of each organization

practical tip

professionals—we revel in the "small print" explanations and disclaimers. And if we don't like them, we at least respect them greatly. The time to discuss and agree on these issues is in the planning stages, not in the postaward phase.

Grant Summary Form

We're not about killing trees with extra paperwork, but a strong grant summary form can prove very useful. It should contain the following items:

◆ Name of funder

◆ Lead agency (if applicable)

◆ Key personnel and responsibilities of each

◆ Due dates of key activities (reports due, etc.)

◆ Project owner/monitor

◆ Amount of award

 practical tip

---

Many grant professionals use a one-page grant summary form that outlines key accountabilities for the project. The summary form serves as the one place that everyone can reference for basic information on the project and funding. Of course, signatures from all key personnel should be included to prevent "I was not aware of that" down the road. One person, either the grant professional or the project director, should monitor the progress and provide periodic check-ins during the grant cycle. This information should be specified in the summary form.

During the grant cycle, the project monitor must regularly check in with all key personnel. Some of this can happen through email, but it's always better to include face-to-face meetings as well. For example, if the project will be monitored quarterly, the organizer should call a meeting before the quarterly report is due. We recommend providing free food as a shameless incentive to encourage attendance. Please note that this technique is less effective for phone or video conference calls.

At a face-to-face check-in meeting, everyone brings data needed for the report (client numbers, deliverables met or unmet, and financial records). It's also easier to recap where the project is against the original plan. If spending or deliverables are not on track, team members can address problems and put an improvement plan in place. Keep the presentation materials in your files for later reference or in case the funder wants to audit your organization.

Logic Models

The logic model is an essential part of effective project design. It's also a term that causes many grant professionals to gnash their teeth and pull out their hair. But once mastered, logic models will make your life much easier. Really!

While many versions of the logic model are available, they all consist of a few basic parts: inputs, activities, outputs, and objectives. Let's look at each of these in more detail.

Inputs are the elements needed to make the project work. This could be staff, clients, money, space, technology, or equipment. Think about all of the pieces your project needs. Is your project focused on starting a tutoring program? If so, your inputs would be tutors, students, space to tutor in, and tutoring supplies (books, paper, pencils, calculators, etc.). You may also want to include incentives for the students to attend or to reward them for meeting milestones. Do you need to consider transportation? How will your students get to the program? This may prompt you to include bus tokens or mileage reimbursement if the tutors are working with students in their students' homes.

Let's look at another example. Maybe a local police department wants to build capacity of its organization by increasing technology. Adding new computers to the patrol cars may be the element needed to improve response times or accuracy. Inputs might include the new computers, instructors to train the officers on how to use the computers, and IT personnel to install and manage the new technology.

Inputs will also help in creating the project budget. Make sure the items listed in your logic model and project narrative are included in the project budget, and vice versa. It's easy to lose track of this correlation in the heat of a daunting deadline, but matching up the logic model and narrative to the budget is a key component of a strong proposal. You can also use the cross-matching process to help guide practical discussions of the project budget with the design team.

> ### Inputs
>
> *Inputs* are those items needed for the implementation of the project. These can be staff, clients, space, equipment, bus tokens, etc.
>
>

Activities will use the inputs to achieve the outputs and outcomes. If you think about a logic model as a recipe, the activities are the directions (mix, add, stir, blend, etc.). Using our tutoring example, the activities include hiring tutors, recruiting students, purchasing supplies/equipment, providing the tutoring, and evaluating student progress. In the police department example, activities may be purchasing the technology, installing the computers in the cars, training officers to use the computers, and evaluating the changes in reporting or community enforcement after using the new computers. This section will inform the methodology of the project proposal.

> ### Activities and Outputs
>
> *Activities* are the things your project will do to meet the goals and objectives of the project. This can include hiring staff, securing contracts, providing a service, collecting data, etc.
>
> *Outputs* are the results of activities and are sometimes thought of as process objectives. They're defined by the ability to quantify or count them.
>
>

Outputs are what result from the activities. In the tutoring example, the outputs may be five tutors hired, twenty-five students recruited, and 250 hours of tutoring provided.

Sometimes confused with outcomes or objectives, outputs are what happen from the results of our logic model recipe (the shaking, stirring, and pureeing). The outputs from our police department example could be new computers installed in all police cars and thirty officers trained in using the new technology. This would equate to the finished product in our recipe example. The cake or cookies are baked and ready to eat. Or maybe the doughnuts.

The outcomes section of the logic model is often divided into two or three subsections. They include short-term, midterm, and long-term outcomes, although some models only use two (usually short-term and either long- or midterm).

The *objectives* are the changes that you expect to happen as a result of the project. In the short term, you might expect the students to be retained in the tutoring program for at least three months and for those students to have demonstrated improvement by one-half grade level in one subject area.

The length of time used in the short-term, midterm, and long-term objectives is not set in stone, but is relative to the project. Generally, most short-term objectives are approximately six months to one year. Assuming our tutoring project spans one school year, the short-term objectives may be measured at the semester while the midterm objectives may be measured at year end. Long-term objectives reflect the changes you want to see in the lives of your clients and often span several years.

In using our police department example, the short-term objectives may be to have all officers demonstrate proficiency in using the new technology and to have officers able to respond to calls more accurately in the first six months of use. The midterm objective may be that response times are reduced by a certain percentage, a reduced number of errors in information received from dispatch, and an increase in the satisfaction of the community from officers using better technology.

Use of Terms

Funders and organizations often use the terms *goals* and *objectives* interchangeably. For our purposes, goals are the overarching ideal you want clients to achieve. Objectives are the milestones to assure you are getting there. However, you should use the terms in the way defined by the funder.

important

Contrary to popular opinion in the grants world, logic models are not inherently evil or a cruel joke from heartless funders! Actually, the logic model is the one document that meets the needs of everyone on the project team. As the grant professional, you have the information necessary to construct the proposal; as the project director, you have the roadmap for implementation; and as the evaluator, you have the measures necessary to prove success.

Elements of Project Design

The elements of the project are all designed to work together as described in the logic model. While funders may use many of the terms interchangeably, we'll stick with those outlined above. The project goal is the long-term, overarching theme of the project—the ideal state when the project is successful, and usually several years down the road. The goal is our destination.

Objectives are the measurements to let us know we're following the correct route. If the goal is that youth in our community are reading at grade level by the fourth grade, then our objectives should let us know if we're on the right path. It may be that youth enrolled in our tutoring program make certain gains by a set of due dates (increase reading level by one grade level within six months of tutoring or pass reading skill level tests at set intervals). Objectives are what happen as a result of the outputs and activities.

All of these goals and objectives are measured through project evaluation. The evaluation plan is the assessment and action steps that are undertaken to ensure the project worked or didn't work. It defines what we're planning to measure (due dates, timelines met, and improvement in the lives of clients, growth, or skills attainment), as well as how and when we will measure these items. This may include providing a pretest and post-test evaluation after clients receive some type of training or education, satisfaction surveys, tests or knowledge change measurement, or skills evaluation.

Defining what tools are to be used and when the measurements will be taken is an important step. We can't just say that clients will improve because of our project; we must be able to define and prove the kind of improvement expected. The evaluation plan clearly describes what we're looking for and how we'll know if we got there.

Evaluation Data

How do we know if our evaluation plan is sound? It must include measures beyond output or activity measures and satisfaction. As stated earlier in this chapter, output measures describe the activities, not the results. True project evaluation includes measurement that describes how the clients' lives are better because of the intervention they received. Have students gained grade levels in reading or math? Have individuals diagnosed with HIV been able to lead healthier lives because they are engaged in ongoing treatment? Is the community safer because police officers are able to respond to emergencies faster and more accurately with new technology?

Using qualitative and quantitative data are the best ways to measure impact. Quantitative data refers to what you can count: how many, how much, and by what increase or decrease. These are important indicators of growth that are more easily obtained.

Qualitative data is trickier and often stumps project teams and grant professionals. It refers to *why* the change matters. Using focus groups, interviews, and questionnaires/surveys are some methods to get this information.

Qualitative data provides the meaning (why) behind the changes (what). Another way to think of this is to measure the improvement in clients' lives because they participated in your program.

For example, why do we care if students learn to read better or if police are able to respond better to calls? The ultimate answer is because it affects the human condition and improves our communities. Qualitative data provides the context for how our projects and programs address these big-picture concepts.

For instance, describing the positive changes in a child's life once that student can read at grade level tells a far better story than only reporting a test score. Since a single grant doesn't last forever, these stories provide a rich source of information for donor appeals, future grant proposals, marketing, and organization newsletters.

> ### What's Your Evaluation Plan?
>
> The evaluation plan is not just a restated methodology plan with a column for evidence. This happens quite often in proposals. It's also not a short paragraph promising that an evaluation of some sort may indeed take place sometime.
>
> Evaluation plans are well thought out and clearly define what measures will be taken, when they will happen, and who's responsible. Be sure to include estimated dates for analysis and sharing of information.
>
> watch out!

Eventually, statistical data can help prove the success of your project. Since statistics are usually lagging indicators over several years, they're not often used in an annual report to a funder. But over time, most projects should be measurable through statistics. Showing the changes in the percentage of students referred to the principal's office for disciplinary reasons, or the percentage of students who are considered chronically truant after your intervention compared to before your intervention, is a powerful statement. It moves beyond individual change to demonstrate systemic changes and leads to a better learning environment.

Incorporating Community Resources

We've already discussed many aspects of creating a collaborative project plan. Where do you get started? Since each community is unique, we can't give you an exhaustive list of resources, but here are a few places to get you started.

Think about the problem you're trying to address and create a list of those organizations that can provide a part of the solution.

Each community usually has some general organizing bodies that can help you identify other organizations. The local United Way is often a clearinghouse of nonprofit agencies that serve diverse groups of clients. Schools are also organized around education service centers and county or state boards of education. Most counties also have boards of health, boards of mental health, human services, and children's services. Don't forget to check with relevant local and state agencies as well.

Foundations and other funders, because of their own strong relationships in the nonprofit community, may also be able to help you connect with like-minded organizations for collaborative work.

These all are good starting places for finding out what other organizations are doing. Of course, an Internet search will also provide a nice resource list. Your professional network will be another good resource. Yet another reason to go out and meet new people!

Sustainability

Everyone asks for it and we all struggle with it. Quick hints here: a one-sentence sustainability plan that focuses only on writing more grants won't win friends or influence funders. The weekly purchase of lottery tickets is also not a super strong sustainability plan. You're welcome!

Seriously, though, even if the funder you're applying to doesn't require a sustainability plan, addressing it up front with the project design team and in the proposal will only help your case.

The bottom line of sustainability is the question: How do you plan to pay for your project going forward? A good evaluation plan with quantitative and qualitative data will provide an enticing story to draw in new, private donations. However, your organization has probably grown dependent on certain donors, even though you should not expect continued project funds from these groups. So where else can you expect to receive funds?

Can you charge a fee for your program? Even a small amount of money from each client may help to offset the cost of the project. This will also show future grant funders that the clients have a stake in the game. Having other revenue-producing ventures in your organization can help. Can you rent space or sell back office support to other organizations? Can you provide training to other organizations in your area of expertise and charge a fee to offset the costs of the project?

More and more nonprofit organizations are seeking creative ways to fund themselves. In one local community, a small nonprofit that provides training and assistance to individuals who are considered unemployable also runs a small pizza parlor. The pizza parlor is a place where the clients learn job skills and the profits go to fund the education and training program.

Maybe your project is unique, and you can seek organizations in other communities to pay you to teach them how to replicate your project. Think creatively and you'll be able to find solutions to sustainability.

Are You Exam Ready?

You are exam ready if you can identify:

◆ Ways to solicit and incorporate meaningful input and contributions by stakeholders, including client groups, beginning with the development of a new concept or program

◆ Ways to build partnerships and facilitate collaborations among applicants

◆ Strategies to educate grant applicants about financial and programmatic accountability to comply with funder requirements

◆ The structure, value, and applications of logic models as they relate to elements of project design

◆ Definitions of and interrelationships among elements of project design (e.g., project goals, objectives, activities, evaluation)

◆ Design and development decisions that are data-based (e.g., descriptive, qualitative, environmental, statistical)

◆ Community resources that aid in developing programs and projects

◆ The impact of solid evaluation designs on the success and sustainability of your project or program

Chapter Four

Grant Proposal Development

IN THIS CHAPTER

- ···➔ Grant application guidelines

- ···➔ Parts of the proposal

- ···➔ Appropriate proposal-writing approaches

- ···➔ Submitting proposals electronically

Do you know how to craft, construct, and submit an effective grant application? In this chapter, we consider the fourth GPCI competency and the associated skills.

One brutal truth of how to prepare an effective grant application is that the writing itself isn't the most important part. Soaring prose, heart-tugging success stories, and metaphors that would move the most cynical reviewer to tears are useless if your proposal doesn't follow the rules of RFP guidelines and requirements, arrives after the deadline, or is lost in cyberspace because of an unforeseen snafu with a server or power outage.

Just like news stories of the 104-year-old who sips bourbon and smokes cigars every day, there are tales of grant professionals who wait until the last minute and produce a high-quality, award-winning, and program-saving behemoth of a proposal. Both the tippling elder and the last-minute marvel are the exceptions, not the rule.

Crafting and submitting an effective grant application means understanding the application requirements and then building in enough time to gather required data while also writing clearly, concisely, and compellingly. As online grant submissions and character counts (including spaces, of course) emerge as the new normal for submitting grant applications, organizing up front is vital to your success as a grant professional.

Your reading comprehension skills will help you be successful with writing and submitting grants long before you type the first word onto a blank application. A thirty-page federal RFP and a two-paragraph web page from a new family foundation may not seem like they have a lot in common, but they often describe the basic components designed to help your application succeed—believe it or not!

Grant Application Guidelines

Scan the application first to make sure your organization qualifies to submit an application and that the deadline is feasible for the amount of information needed to complete the grant request. For example, you don't want to jump into a fifty-page federal application only to find out days later that your organization isn't even in one of the states qualified to apply. It's tempting to skim the RFP to get to the "good parts" first—like funding amounts and award ranges. But you may miss another important prerequisite, like a maximum organizational budget needed to apply or a fully developed strategic plan you need to include with the attachments.

Grant Application

Grant proposal materials include the grant application form, funder guidelines, and legislative rules for application submission. The materials are also known as the RFP, NOFA, or call for proposals. The grant application is the applicant's response.

You don't want to spend hours writing a grant proposal if your organization can't produce the required documents and attachments by the application's deadline. Thoroughly read and review the application requirements. Many funders provide budget templates or may require copies of 990s, audited financials, strategic plans, or letters of support. The time to understand all those requirements is well before you begin writing the grant proposal, not three hours before the deadline.

Taking time at the beginning of the application process to review all the requirements of the application is essential to preparing an effective application. Scoring rubrics or point values may be included in the RFP. Use these values to help define how you approach the application. To revisit the movie director simile, consider the higher point valued questions as the biggest "scenes" of your application. Your section on "sustainability" may be the grant application equivalent of a climactic battle for world domination in a summer blockbuster, taking the most time and talent in your working budget. (Only you probably won't be working with giant robots, enormous special effects teams, or movie stars!) In other words, prepare to spend the most time on the sections of the application worth the most points.

Elements of Standard Grant Proposal Applications

A standard grant proposal includes an abstract, needs assessment, mission and organizational history, project narrative, objectives, activities, action plans, budgets and budget narratives, future funding/sustainability statements, and evaluation plan.

Abstract or Executive Summary

An RFP will often include a request for an executive summary, abstract, summary cover letter, or another similar document for your application. Even though

---

Reading is Fundamental!

Reading the full RFP and application guidelines will prevent you from spending a lot of time working on a proposal when your organization doesn't qualify.

---

it most likely appears first on the list of application requirements, don't write it first. In fact, the summary should be the last thing you write. If it helps, think of the application process as like directing a movie. Rarely, if ever, does the making of a movie mean shooting the script in order. Travel schedules, location availability, weather, production budget, temperamental talent, and paparazzi invasions may all factor into the film's shooting schedule. But the end product follows the beginning, middle, and end arc of storytelling. And those trailers you see before the main feature starts? They're not shot until the end of film production—it's hard to pull the most thrilling highlights from footage that hasn't yet been filmed. So consider yourself the "director" of the grant application process, and know that "first billing" in a grant application doesn't necessarily mean first written.

Federal applications and those from larger foundations may provide a specific form and/or have a strict word or character count for an abstract or summary. Otherwise, assume that your summary should run somewhere between 250 to 500 words, or one-page maximum. Think of it as the "trailer" or "highlight reel" of your grant application.

An effective summary should include what problem or issue your project or program will solve, how it works, and what the outcomes will be. End with the total project budget and the requested amount from the funder. If it isn't requested in other parts of the application, this is also the place to include your mission statement, location, project name, and contact information. Some funders may request this information in advance through a cover letter or letter of intent.

Problem Statements

Problem statements, also referred to as *needs assessments* or *needs for program*, are common titles of a key proposal section where the funder wants to understand the macro and micro levels of the problem or issue that your program will solve if funded. Carefully consider the audience for this proposal as you gather the data to support your case. For example, if you're writing a proposal about a local no-kill pet shelter to the corporate foundation of an international pet food manufacturer, the reviewers are more likely to know about the plight of unwanted pets than if you were seeking funding for the same program from a local family foundation for the first time.

In short, let the audience/potential reviewers determine how you best present the facts that describe the need for the program. Too often, grant professionals feel compelled to cram every fact and data point they've ever found into a clump of numbers or percentages. At best, this statistical overkill is hard to follow. At worst, it can defeat the best-intentioned proposal before it barely gets started. Here are some key points to consider when putting together your need statement.

Think Globally but Source Locally

Search for the most localized data possible about whatever global condition the program would solve. For example, an effective need statement for a community food pantry should include the hunger and poverty statistics of the area it serves. No need to waste precious line space on global poverty, or over-explaining that not having enough nutritious food is bad for the human body. Focus instead on census data on poverty or hunger and on state, regional, and/or local data from respected national or international government or nonprofit organizations.

> **When Should You Write the Summary or Project Abstract?**
>
> The summary or project abstract should be written last after all of the other parts of the application are completed. Having written the full proposal, you now have the key information necessary to summarize the work.
>
> practical tip

Don't Data Dump

Choose your supporting facts carefully and then consider ways to make them even more compelling through comparisons. There may be so many impoverished elderly in your city that if brought together they would fill every seat in the local sports stadium. Or there may be enough trash clogging a local waterway to fill four tractor-trailer rigs. Use relatable images to tell your story based on the hard data gathered in advance. Painting a picture for the reader or reviewer will be far more compelling than simply a bunch of numbers or figures. You want to get the reviewers' attention, not put them to sleep.

Back It Up

Keep an organized record of every statistic cited in your proposal. Word or character limits may preclude longer, more academic style citations in the original proposal, but keep copies or at least URLs for studies and statistics used to build the need statement. Reviewers or program officers not familiar with the most recent research may have follow-up questions or want to read the original research. Have a list of sources and citations ready to share.

Organization Mission and History

Many grant applications ask for your organization's mission and history. Make sure the information included really supports your case. Don't just cut and paste tired boilerplate from a brochure or website. State the organization's mission as succinctly as possible and then focus on key developments, awards, programs, and transitions that show history, progress, growth in numbers served, or other positive developments. It's good practice to keep a timeline on file of key organizational history accomplishments. Making sure that your organization has a succinct mission statement can make grant proposal preparation faster. If there's no mission statement, then work with organizational leadership to develop one before beginning the grant application. This can be a time-consuming but effective way to build capacity for future proposals.

Your organization's history is important to show that you have the expertise in addressing the problem your program will mitigate. This can be a bit tricky. You don't want to give a long, boring history of how Mr. and Mrs. Smith founded the organization long ago, but you do want to demonstrate how your organization is *the* one that can address the need in the community. Focus on key successes and milestones.

What if your organization is new and doesn't have much history? Good question. If that's the case, we suggest you focus on the history of the key personnel or why the organization was founded. What are you doing that other organizations are not?

Proposal/Project Narrative

Whether it's five pages or a five-hundred character limit, the proposal/project narrative section most closely follows the standard journalism credo of the five W's and the H— who, what, when, where, why and how. The *who* is the targeted audience or client of the program. Who will benefit from your program? Why are these individuals or this group the best audience to address? We suggest being very deliberate about the target audience so the reviewers clearly know you are trying to effect change by serving those who need your service. You aren't casting a wide net—you're fishing for a specific species of fish.

The *what* will most likely form the bulk of this section, covering the basic structure of the program or project that will solve the problem or meet the need described in the problem statement. The five W's and the H are not intended as actual written sections of the narrative, but as a conceptual

framework for covering the most essential elements of a well-constructed narrative.

Entire series of books, classes, webinars, and courses provide hours of instruction focused only on the actual writing—a worthy subject beyond the scope of this manual. However, three basic rules of good grant writing (or any good writing at all) are worth remembering:

Use active rather than passive voice whenever possible. *Passive* voice isn't wrong, but *active* voice can explain your ideas more clearly, especially when space is limited to express your ideas. A passive sentence is, "The program is designed to provide participants with knowledge of basic nutritional practices." An active version is, "Participants will learn about basic nutritional practices." Not only is the active voice more intriguing, but it's more powerful and shorter.

Mixing simple, compound, and complex sentences makes the narrative easier to follow and understand. To review, a simple sentence contains a subject and verb and expresses a complete thought. For example, "The 5th Street Shelter opened in 1980" is a simple sentence.

A compound sentence contains two independent clauses joined by a word such as *and, but, or, for, nor, yet,* or *so.* Here's an example: "The Community Center has more than five hundred members, *and* it provides a wide variety of health and wellness programs."

Finally, a complex sentence includes an independent clause joined by at least one dependent clause that is set off with a "subordinator," such as *when, because, since,* or *although,* or with a relative pronoun such as *who, which,* or *that.* Here's an example: "*Although* the animal shelter is located on twelve acres of fenced property, the growing number of unwanted larger animals has pushed the shelter to the maximum number of inhabitants."

The project narrative should include the major components of the program—the "what" of this section. Whenever possible, describe the program in order of its occurrence without getting bogged down in every detail. "A series of weekly parenting classes" can convey the crux of the setup without going into the specific time and day of the week. Thoughtful condensing of program details is especially important for applications with space limitations. They also keep the interest of your reader. You don't want reviewers checking out or going to sleep reading your proposal, do you?

When should be a brief mention of the length of the proposed program. Your program or project start and end dates will unlikely coincide directly with a foundation's particular funding cycle. But make sure that your project timeline includes reportable activities that fall within their own funding timeline. For example, if you're planning a capital construction project that will take three to five years to complete, make sure there are concrete, measurable activities that will be fundable and fall within the usually shorter grant cycle. Make sure the narrative also includes *where* the project or program will take place.

Active Voice

Using an active voice and mixing complex and simple sentences are key ways to add depth to your proposal. These techniques create a more powerful message.

Mention of the *why* of the program can appear throughout the narrative according to descriptions of the individual components, and is closely connected to the *how* of the project. For example, "Daily, healthy meals and snacks at the Senior Center will provide a gathering point for informal discussions with participants about what they eat at home." The previous sentence is an example of the *what, when,* and *how* of a program that has a component of needs assessment for nutrition among low-income seniors. Keep in mind that the five W's and an H can also help you construct individual sentences or sections of the narrative, which is especially useful for complex, multisite programs.

Well-produced photos, infographics, charts, tables, and graphs can add visual interest to proposals when space permits. Including a brief anecdote or pithy quote from a participant or client can help reviewers connect with the project and/or program. Use a chart that compares achievements of programs from year to year, or a bar graph of program participation, to summarize information quickly. These additions put a face to the statistics and other program data and can help tell the story of why your project deserves funding. In longer program narratives, a summary chart or photo can also visually break up the proposal, making for an easier, more enjoyable read for the review committee members. Always review application guidelines first to make sure such photos or graphics are okay to include.

Including extra materials is often impossible with online applications. Increasingly popular through third-party providers like CyberGrants, or through proprietary sites set up by funders themselves, online applications usually include the same essential components as traditional proposals. The convenience and immediacy of submitting proposals online also brings some challenges unique to this growing medium.

Online applications usually have shorter, stricter word counts or even character counts, as well as requirements to upload supporting documents. Often, these applications have automatic cut-offs for maximum word or character (letters and the spaces between them) limits. Spell checks are not always featured in online applications. We recommend that you create a word processing document following the sections of the online application and use it to create drafts. Use word/character counts, spell check, and other features in this draft document and then cut and paste into the online application.

Don't think you can procrastinate just because you're submitting online. Networks crash, browsers may not support the easy uploading of attachments,

---

When Should I Include Additional Materials?

On a related note, only include annual reports, brochures, or other additional materials when requested, or if there is a section for additional information such as an appendix. Remember that reviewers may be faced with dozens or even hundreds of proposals to review. Exceeding word limits or sending extra, unrequested information could actually disqualify your proposal rather than help state your case for funding.

observation

and too many applicants right at deadline may overload the online portal. Don't leave online applications to the last minute!

Objectives, Activities, and Action Plans

Objectives, activities, and action plans may be separate components of a proposal or part of your program narrative. They may also be separate worksheets or attachments in more complex proposals. To further complicate things, funders may use these words interchangeably, or use close approximations such as *goals*, *strategies*, and *tactics*. Again, make sure to review the entire RFP thoroughly before you write the first word. This will go a long way in helping you define and direct the grant proposal writing process. Make sure you understand what the funder means by these terms. The definitions we use in this manual are not meant to supersede any specifics given directly by an individual funder.

Objectives

Objectives are short sentences or phrases that describe the major projected accomplishments of the program. Think of them as "mini" five W's and an H (who, what, when, where, why, and how) for each major activity. Successfully written objectives should be **s**imple, **m**easurable, **a**ttainable, **r**ealistic, and **t**ime-bound, or *SMART*. They describe the changes that will be made once your project is successfully implemented.

Goals versus Objectives

A *goal* is the overall purpose of the project or program. This is a large, often long-term, ideal.

The *objectives* are the collection of steps to be taken or achieved by the project or program. The objectives are very concrete and structured.

Here's an example: "At least 80 percent of elementary school students completing the twelve-month 'Music and More' afterschool program at the Elm District Youth Center will show more than 30 percent improvement in music skills demonstrations." A weaker objective is, "Students enrolled in 'Music and More' will learn to play their instruments." Clearly, the second example lacks the specificity, time boundaries, and measurable outcomes of the first example.

The more specific your objectives are, the easier they will be to report on. Getting the funding and then not being able to report on the work is a terrible predicament. Everyone involved in the project should easily be able to tell if it's successful. The reviewer, the funder, and the project implementation team should all be on the same page and have the same expectations. If you have clear objectives, it helps the implementation or project team to know whether or not they're on track. If they review the project quarterly, for example, they should know if the project is working as intended or if changes need to be made. Waiting until the end of the project or funding year is a bad time to find out that your program didn't have the desired results. Not only is this embarrassing, it puts your organization in jeopardy of future funding. Just as you taste your dish as you're making it to ensure it's seasoned correctly, you should also check your program periodically. You'd hate to wait until your guests are eating dinner to find out that you replaced sugar with salt accidentally. Blech!

Activities

The activities section most commonly lists the primary steps to accomplishing the objectives. This is sometimes called the methodology. In the previous example of the children's music class, activities could include the actual components of the classes such as listening to music, taking field trips to classical concerts, or total minutes of class practice time. Again, a specific request for a list of activities may not appear in a shorter application. You could include a class description or other list of activities as an attachment, or place it in a section that asks you to include any extra information not covered in the main body of the application. A note of caution here: Only include attachments that are permissible by the funder. You don't want to waste time including attachments that will be thrown out.

Action Plans or Timelines

Funders often want you to list or briefly explain when the main parts of the programs or projects will take place throughout the grant cycle. They may want you to provide action plans, timelines, or milestones. Longer, more complex proposals may provide specific forms for this information. If not, you can give them a basic timeline that shows months or quarters and a brief description of key happenings in each time period. This section tells the funder and reviewers that you've given careful consideration to the activities, when they will occur, and who's responsible for getting them completed. This is not the place to be vague. Let the funder know you've thought of everything.

Adding Visual Interest

Using bars, graphs, and pictures can add visual diversity and other interest to your proposal. They help break up long passages of text and compile large amounts of information into a manageable bite.

Effective Budgets and Budget Narratives

Budgets are almost never requested first in a typical application. Grant professionals who come to grant writing through a love of language tend to shy away from budget creation, instead leaving it to program or finance staff or making it the last thing they tackle in the proposal. However, most reviewers turn to budgets first, as a well-constructed budget can quickly explain the crux of the program and its costs.

An incomplete or weakly constructed budget could easily jeopardize all of the hard work you put in on the program narrative and the rest of the application. Returning to the movie director image at the start of this chapter, remember that the most well-constructed grant applications are often composed out of order. So, focusing on the budget first and crafting a well-ordered, detailed list of program expenses can help drive the objectives, program narrative, and evaluation of the proposal.

This section refers to "budgets" as program or project-related budgets rather than an overall organization budget. Of course, if the proposal calls for general operating support, then an organization budget covering a fiscal year that is board-approved should be included. Your organization's budget should include projected revenues and expenses in major categories such as salaries, benefits, program expenses, and supplies, and standard operational categories such as telecommunications, postage, facilities, and utilities. This is by no means an exhaustive list, just a brief overview.

In some cases, a funder may provide a specific form to use rather than accepting the prepared operational budget developed by the finance department. The categories provided may not exactly match those of your organization—another reason to allow plenty of time for proposal review and to develop a clear understanding of budget components—and to work closely with the finance department!

Project budgets will almost always require you to start from scratch and collaborate with program and finance staff members. You should begin to do this as soon after your initial RFP review as possible. Follow the form provided or include the basic components mentioned in the description of the organizational budget. Spreadsheet applications such as Excel are easy to format and export if needed. Make sure to write brief descriptions for each line item, and remember that the budget should function as a stand-alone overview of the entire proposal.

You should also carefully review the allowable and nonallowable costs of the RFP and make sure that your program or project budget aligns with what they will fund. In federal grants, for instance, most costs related to food, such as refreshments for class or meetings aren't allowable. For many funders, only direct program costs are allowable. These direct program costs may exclude salaries and benefits of program staff, but could include training materials and supplies needed to carry out the program.

The expenses associated with administrative staff, utilities, costs related to maintaining the building or program site, telecommunications, and other such costs are often grouped into a proposal budget category called overhead, indirect costs, or facilities and administrative costs. Not every funder will cover these expenses even though they are legitimate program costs. If your organization has a large amount of funding, particularly federal grants, you may have a negotiated indirect cost rate. Be careful with indirect costs. Sometimes, items such as utilities and phones are considered direct costs. Always check the RFP guidelines or ask the program officer what's allowed or not allowed.

When building a project budget for a funder that won't award grant dollars for indirect costs, simply include these costs in the budget and indicate that the indirect costs or the nonallowable costs will be covered by another revenue source. Just make sure to only account for the portion of rent, utilities, or other such categories used by the project—not for the organization as a whole. You'll need to explain how you got to this figure in the budget narrative. As long as you apply the formula to all costs, your budget should be accepted. However, this is an area often missed by applicants.

Other revenue sources are also important for government and other grant funding that calls for matching funds. Again, the RFP, especially the sections on budget preparation, should specify if the grant requires matching funds. Matching funding means that your organization must contribute its own funds to the project in order to receive the grant funding. Many federal or state RFPs require matching funds. You'll need to explain clearly where these matching funds will come from or your plan for raising matching dollars.

Some requests for proposals may extend the matching funds concept to include documented volunteer hours, the value of capital equipment, in-kind donations, and other sources. If your organization isn't able to provide evidence of matching funds, don't waste your time and resources completing the proposal.

Budget Narrative

The budget narrative, sometimes called the budget justification, is the place where you can explain all of the costs or expenses listed in your budget form. Some funders have a specific format they want you to use. If not, you can simply follow the logical flow of each line in the budget and explain why these costs are reasonable. If you have staff members included in the budget, list their titles, explain their duties or responsibilities in the project, list the percentage of their time on the project, and who they report to. This is also the place to explain how you derived the percentages of rent and other larger costs assigned to the project. If the portion of the rent used in the project is based on the percentage of FTEs (full-time equivalents) working on the project, then give the formula and apply it across other budget lines. You should also list how you came up with other expenses listed. Instead of simply listing $240 for various

---

Matching Funds

For example, a $250,000 request for firefighter safety equipment could require that the county or city provide evidence that they have an additional $250,000 from a nonfederal source to cover the balance of the equipment purchase.

Example

office supplies, you should list the cost based on $20 per month times twelve months. Better yet, list the items you're going to purchase (books, paper, curricula, etc.) and the cost per item. The more specific you are, the better the funder will feel about investing in you.

Future Funding/Sustainability Statements

Future funding/sustainability statements are the sections where you explain how the program or project will continue after the grant funding ends. The more specific you are, the better. No funder wants to read that your organization will continue to seek additional grants in the future, or that you are planning to raise more money soon. Be prepared to list specific funding commitments either pledged or received. Include the amount and the name of the funder. Just like showing evidence of matching funds, a complete, well-written sustainability statement helps assure the funder that their grant funds will be well stewarded. If you can show concrete plans to continue a program and project that are not dependent on a single source of funds, you'll have a better chance of attracting grants.

Some applications also require other evidence of an organization's financial well-being, such as the percentage of board giving and the total dollars contributed by the board of directors in the current fiscal year. For the same reason, documents such as audited financials, organizational budgets, and projected budgets versus year-to-date actual expenses and revenues are often requested as additional evidence of an organization's financial stability.

Evaluation Models

Your proposal's evaluation models also show a funder that your organization has specific plans to continue a program or project beyond a single grant award. One of the most common mistakes in developing an evaluation model is to only include numbers served or to track attendance. These measures, or process evaluations, could form a component of an overall evaluation model, but this would be weak as the only item presented in the evaluation section.

Basic evaluation models include formative, process, and outcome evaluation. Formative evaluation is especially important for developing new programs and projects. Common methods include stakeholder interviews, town hall meetings and data/literature reviews. Process evaluation calls for measuring and evaluating if your project did what it was supposed to do. You could use town hall meetings, focus groups, and opinion surveys to measure how well a project is meeting the expectations of the target audience it serves. Employee or satisfaction surveys, class or conference evaluation forms, and exit interviews are examples of formative evaluation measures appropriate to established programs or projects.

Outcome evaluation tracks measurable changes in participants or projects throughout the cycle of the given funded program. These are sometimes referred to as *impact objectives*. These evaluation measures are typically the most difficult and expensive to implement, but they're most attractive to funders. For example, drops in cholesterol levels of seniors completing cardiac rehabilitation programs, increases in high school graduation rates, and decreases in dangerous chemicals in local water supplies are outcome evaluation measures. Smaller scale measures could include statistically significant changes in pretests and posttests of knowledge following a nutrition course or in a series of fitness tests conducted before and after an intensive athletic training program.

Realistic and measurable outcome evaluation tools are just as important as objectives. Think about them thoughtfully when you're planning and writing your proposal, not at the last minute before a proposal deadline. This is especially important when working with third-party evaluators. Larger programs, medical/clinical trials, or scientific research may also require third-party evaluations.

Third-party evaluators are not always as fun as they sound, but evaluators are a critical part of the grant application process. These people are external, independent professionals who are responsible for designing the methods and processes used to assess the outcomes and outputs of the grant-funded project or program.

The interesting thing about third-party evaluators is that their fee might be an allowable expenditure. They are responsible for evaluating the program/project and the very grant that pays their invoices. With federal grants from the US Department of Education, the program evaluation component can range up to 20 percent of the total grant budget. The irony of being paid by the grant to evaluate the grant's outcome is difficult to overlook. The value of the third-party relationship is important to protect the integrity of the program research.

Submitting Proposals Electronically

It seems as if every funder accepts grant proposals electronically. A few ask for one original copy of the application and a digital file copy. Some want a CD-ROM with the digital copy and others will accept the entire application via email. Many more funders have moved to online electronic submissions via a branded portal they host on their website. This trend has resulted in new and interesting strategies.

For one, submission deadlines have changed. In the past, for example, a proposal needed to be postmarked on or before November 5. Now, you must submit the proposal online before 11:59 p.m., November 5, Eastern Standard Time. This can give you a few extra hours of work time if you work in the Eastern Time zone, or three hours less if you work in the Pacific Time zone. No system is the best for everyone.

The strategy for submitting your application should include writing the content off-line. Why? Because servers crash, power loss occurs, Internet providers go out of business, and a whole host of other reasons. You should draft the content in a text or Word document and cut and paste it into the online application portal. Also, some online products don't let you save and return later. If the portal allows you to save your work, do so often. Why? Because if the server doesn't crash, it could time out and erase all of your content before you can submit it online.

Program Evaluation

Program evaluation is a methodology for collecting, analyzing, and using data to answer fundamental questions about projects, policies, and programs particular to grant-funded programs. Effective program evaluation is a systematic way to improve and account for inputs, outcomes, and throughputs. The result of program evaluation is a report of findings and measurements.

The cool thing about a quality program evaluation by an experienced evaluator is that a grant professional can use the results to seek program continuation funding. Program evaluations answer the basic question: did the grant funds make an impact? Good evaluators can provide a grant professional with a roadmap for additional grant submissions down the line.

Submit Early

We, of course, recommend submitting your grant application at least a day early. Why? Because servers crash, buildings lose power, and the flu can keep grant professionals otherwise occupied.

Are You Exam Ready?

You are exam ready if you can:

◆ Interpret grant application RFP guidelines and requirements to ensure high-quality responses

◆ Identify elements of standard grant proposal applications

◆ Identify work strategies for submitting high-quality proposals on time

◆ Identify accurate and appropriate data sources to support proposal narratives

◆ Identify appropriate, sequential, consistent, and logical presentations of grant narrative elements and ideas among or within proposal components

◆ Identify proposal-writing approaches, styles, tones, and formats appropriate for proposing organizations and various audiences

◆ Identify appropriate and accurate uses of visuals to highlight information

◆ Identify effective practices for developing realistic, accurate line-item and narrative budgets and for expressing the relationship between line items and project activities in the budget narrative

◆ Identify sources of in-kind matches for project budgets

◆ Identify factors that limit how budgets should be developed

◆ Identify evaluation models and components appropriate to grant applications

◆ Identify methods for submitting proposals electronically

Do You Have Online Skills?

Online grant applications require a skill you have to develop. Submitting proposals electronically is a skill with many facets. Stretching your online muscles will serve you well. One critical skill for all grant professionals is using Adobe Acrobat Pro or another software package to create PDF files. Many online grant application portals require you to upload files in PDF format. An online stretching exercise is to practice downloading and uploading files to as many application portals as you can. Most are the same, and some are similar in approach, but a few will throw you for a loop. When a grant deadline is in fifteen minutes, there's no time to learn how to create and upload a PDF file.

practical tip

Chapter Five

Grant Postaward Management

IN THIS CHAPTER

- ···➤ Postaward grant management practices
- ···➤ Regulatory compliance and cost principles
- ···➤ Roles and responsibilities
- ···➤ Effective grant development

Good grant management shows funders that your organization walks its talk. Appropriate implementation of all grant awards leads to more grants for your organization. Best of all, it can change lives for the better as quality programs and services transform communities.

Improper grant management can lead to a loss of funds, loss of future grants, a damaged reputation, or worse—jail time! Knowing how to implement grant projects and/or conduct postaward activities successfully takes time, focus, and attention to detail.

Although you certainly deserve a fun fiesta or at least hearty congratulations after winning a grant, postaward grant management is also an important part of the process. There's a lot of work ahead after you sweep up the confetti and errant champagne corks. You'll need to accept the grant award, set the grant up in your organization's financial management system, hold internal kick-off meetings, deal with vendor and equipment procurement, get internal/external approvals, implement the project, maintain oversight on the progress of the project, report on the project to the funder, and close out the project when you're done.

Your organization may also receive external monitoring or audit visits depending on the type and size of the grant awarded. It's easy to hear the word "audit" and imagine stern-faced IRS bureaucrats knocking on your door. But for most grant professionals, an audit is simply an extended site visit and review of your documentation on the project's finances and outcomes.

Imagine a TV reporter asking the man in the street (or woman in the street) about grants. His first response would most likely be that writing is the most important thing. (We hope that his second response would be to get out of the street.) Most aspiring grant professionals feel the same way. But strong project management skills are crucial to writing and managing grant proposals. The abilities to envision an overall program, gather information from subject-matter experts, to keep a project team on task and on time, and to oversee reporting and funder relations are key to successful grant development and grant management in particular.

Setting up the grant management process for success actually begins before you submit a proposal. Your grant proposal design team should include grant professionals, writers, and program staff to make sure the project can be implemented as it was written in the proposal.

Include appropriate project staff in the planning stages—those who will be tasked with keeping the outcome "promises" made in the application. If the grant's program design was crafted in a vacuum, program staff may struggle to fulfill the goals and activities. Most importantly, communities in need won't benefit from the funds awarded.

Growing your grant management skill set on the job could involve working closely with your finance team to better understand tracking expenses. Skilled program staff may offer valuable insight into what really happens when projects go "boots on the ground." This mentor-mentee relationship can be a powerful on-the-job learning method. If you're a one-person grant shop, consider networking with other grant professionals to find a grant management mentor.

A zombie apocalypse, robots gone rogue, or even glittering vampires have frightened many a moviegoer. But the real horror show for most grant professionals is "Grant Management Gone Wrong." The story begins with a sinking feeling when the grant professional tracks an approaching report deadline and realizes that not a dime has been spent, or invoices have vanished, and outcomes tracking forms have teleported to another dimension.

Grant Postaward Management

Grant postaward management means administering an award from start to finish, from accepting the award to writing the last paragraph of a program outcomes report. The complexity and length of the postaward process is based on the grant amount, length of the grant cycle, and the specific requirements of the granting agency or foundation.

The sinking feeling may turn to terror. And the grant professional (who is a friend of ours, promise) grows desperate. We, ahem... the *anonymous grant professional* first tries to micromanage every single activity of the program team. When that doesn't work, the grant professional flees the scene and doesn't return until after the grant is implemented, hoping for the best. Hours spent in project management training, hours spent recommending project training for program staff... nothing worked for us. Um... we mean *them*—the anonymous grant professional, of course. In a last ditch attempt to save a grant management process in peril, the anonymous grant professional takes on every single aspect of the entire project...and never sleeps again. The horror!

There is a better way. (Cue the hopeful sounds of birds chirping in the rosy dawn!)

The best course of action is to work collaboratively with program staff and the funder to make sure you have the right internal systems and internal controls for your grant project. More often than not, we rely on past successes and seek the advice of our professional network and coworkers. Grant postaward management, or grant project implementation, is something every grant professional should do, at least once.

Postaward Grant Management Practices

In a nutshell, GPCI defines successful postaward grant management as knowing enough about grant management to help create effective grant design and development. Especially if you're not a squirrel, any discussion involving a nutshell may seem a little backwards. (By the way, if you're a literate, grant-writing squirrel, please contact us immediately!)

But seriously, wouldn't you assume that postaward grant management means letting the program staff handle it while you go on to greater grant-writing glory? Well, you know what they say about *assume*, right? That it makes an a** out of you and me? Wait, that didn't exactly come across as we'd planned. Let's try again.

What we're really trying to say is that successful grant management calls for a deep understanding of the cycle of good program design and development that must take place before the grant proposal ever flies out the door, or sails across cyberspace. This competency includes a number of things you should know before you take the GPC exam: standards of regulatory compliance, key functions of grant management, roles and responsibilities of project and management staff, and transition to postaward.

Throughout this chapter, we'll discuss how these practices can lead to effective grant development. Before you read any further, we want to clarify that since we're all GPCs, we're certainly biased about the importance of studying and reviewing for the exam, especially in those areas where you feel like you have the least knowledge or experience. But more importantly, we stake our decades of work on the important concept that the competencies of the GPC exam are also a pathway to effective and efficient service of communities in need. In other words, true grant professionals make things better. Brought a smile to your face, right? It's good work that we're all doing, but it's not easy work.

> ### Working Together for the Common Good
>
> The goals and missions of program staff, development staff, and the funder may differ in key ways, but this group must work together to effectively implement high-quality grant projects. As a grant professional, you should be aware of critical forces at play in postaward management and project implementation.
>
> Remember:
>
> ◆ Everyone is accountable for the outcomes of the grant.
>
> ◆ Internal department "silos" can be dismantled.
>
> ◆ Regular grant meetings can build effective implementation teams.
>
> ◆ Include key project team members such as financial, accounting, and funding source staff in important milestones such as kick-off meetings, ribbon cuttings, and site visits.
>
>
> practical tip

The most important thing is to follow the rules of the grantor. All those struggles in kindergarten to color within the lines may finally pay off for you! As you've no doubt already discovered, grant management doesn't usually involve a box of crayons and a coloring book of puppies and kittens. There's no mandatory naptime, and you're on your own for snacks.

Federal grantmaking agencies' rules are different from the grant management rules of private foundations. State and county grantmakers may require you to follow federal rules, depending on where the grant dollars come from. The origin of the dollars for federal, state, and county grants is often spelled out in the grant application or notice of funding announcement. The same can be said for many private foundation grants. However, private grants may not disclose the source of the funds, and it may not

Are You Experienced?

Use your experience to guide future proposals. Your past grant management experience is the most effective way to inform future successful grant design and development. Ideally, experience would have taught you to be careful what you ask for, as you might just get it!

food for thought

matter anyway. The grantor's program officer may be the only person who knows how the funds need to be managed.

Grant management is both an art and science. The art of it involves building good relationships with program staff, grantors, and other key players. The science part, unfortunately, doesn't involve boiling test tubes or lab coats. It's more about expertly tracking deadlines, clearly defining outcomes, and working together to make sure that all the steps of sound program design are included. To be clear, grant management is impacted by many human factors and many other factors out of our control such as severe weather delays, cash flow needs, and personnel/staffing issues. As you can imagine, implementation is the most unpredictable part of grant management. It's where *life* happens and you make the best of it. Feel free to substitute other, more colorful words for *life*. We won't tell.

Regulatory Compliance

Statutes, regulations, and grant award terms and conditions that apply to grants are typically found in the grant award agreement. Unfortunately, not every grant award has an agreement. When in doubt, ask the funding organization. Don't make us trot out that whole business about *assuming* again; it didn't end well the last time we tried it!

It's your responsibility to know and follow the financial and programmatic procedures, and reporting requirements. Even if you aren't the person who actually performs the program or financial tasks associated with the grant award, you need to know how it all works and be able to explain it well.

To help you out, many federal grantmakers and community foundations host grant implementation workshops and training sessions for grant managers, program staff, and accounting folks. While a lot of them are mandatory, most are not. Make it a priority to promote the schedule and attendance at these workshops and attend all you can. Even the most long-running grant programs change eligibility requirements, funding focus areas, and policies and procedures. Take the time upfront to review them, and you'll have a much smoother grant management process.

Standards of Regulatory Compliance

The standards of regulatory compliance are best summed up as "following the rules."

Remember studying the Watergate scandal from the early '70s? A mysterious informant named "Deep Throat" told intrepid investigative reporters to "follow the money." If you don't remember it or never learned about it in social studies, then go ahead and search for it online. We'll wait.

The whole point of establishing internal controls is that when you or the auditors want to follow the money that flowed in and out of the grant-funded project, it's all there. It's important to have a consistent, well-managed process for handling approvals before grant funds are spent. Proper internal controls are also necessary to track the grant dollars during the reimbursement process. Most federal grants are administered on a reimbursement basis, meaning that the organization must first spend its own funds for the project and then file for reimbursement. In contrast, most grants from corporate or private foundations arrive by check or electronic transfer near the estimated start of the project.

Understanding cash flow management, especially for nonprofits or other organizations without cash reserves, is important in developing sound grant management. Regardless of the type of grant award, you must make sure that your organization can manage grant-funded expenses restricted to specific projects or programs. By manage, we mean maintain procedures that follow generally accepted accounting practices. This doesn't mean putting all the checks into one account, or keeping all the cash in a shoebox under your desk and hoping for the best.

Whether it's a multimillion dollar federal grant, or a $500 check from a local hardware store, you must be able to report accurately on how the money was spent. These reports may be a one-page letter or involve a weeklong site visit by a government auditing team. The same basic rules of sound grant management apply.

Formal audits of grant funds are not always required. For example, the threshold for federal grants is $750,000. The funded organization is subject to an audit under the Single Audit Act if its federal expenditures in a given fiscal year exceed $750,000. This includes federal money that is passed through to states and local entities. Depending on the size of the award, a private foundation may also audit grantees. This is not very common, but it does happen.

More often, funders require financial audits of nonprofits with annual operating budgets larger than $500,000. Third-party accounting firms or other qualified professionals carry out these audits. Having audited financials for your entire

> ### SAM I Am; Green Eggs and Ham?
>
> Even if you're not a fan of Dr. Seuss's children's classic *Green Eggs and Ham,* this is one SAM you should get to know. The System for Award Management (SAM) is the official US government system that consolidated the capabilities of CCR/FedReg, Online Representations and Certifications Application (ORCA), and Excluded Parties List System (EPLS). All entity records from CCR/FedReg and ORCA and exclusion records from EPLS, active or expired, were moved to SAM.
>
> If you don't know SAM, and are not in the mood for green eggs and ham, you should visit its website at *sam.gov.*
>
>  practical tip

organization doesn't mean that it's in trouble. This is not a punitive measure—it's more like annual check-up on the overall health of the organization. Financial audits of nonprofits are often expensive, and funders usually will set a threshold of a minimum operating budget for potential grantees before requiring that they have annual audited financials. Smaller organizations many only need to provide regular financial statements. Consult an accounting professional with significant experience in nonprofit finance for an opinion specific to your agency. And as always, read the grantor's list of required financial documentation and ask questions if necessary.

Understanding contracts and the contracting process at your organization is vital. The organization's procurement policies and requirements must be followed when spending grant funds. Procurement policies and requirements should be at least as rigorous as the federal procurement requirements.

The IRS requires nonprofit organizations of a certain size to file a Form 990 each year. The 990s resemble our beloved income tax forms that we all must complete. But the difference is that nonprofits don't ordinarily pay income taxes, and instead, report on mission, programs, and finances. While this may not sound like exciting bedtime reading, keep in mind that many foundations and individual donors often consult this document to help them decide how to give. And, since most foundations must also regularly submit a public 990, these documents are a great resource for prospect research.

As if this entire topic wasn't already exciting enough, we need to mention a law that governs audit firms in the United States, the Sarbanes-Oxley Act of 2002—more commonly called "Sarbanes-Oxley." Sarbanes-Oxley is a federal law that sets new or enhanced standards for all US public company boards, management, and public accounting firms, requiring auditing departments to first have a comprehensive external audit by a Sarbanes-Oxley compliance specialist to identify areas of risk. Specialized software provides the electronic paper trails necessary to ensure compliance. In many respects, security underpins the requirements of the Sarbanes-Oxley Act. It's the ultimate "follow the money" requirement. It also means that auditing firms have credible and detailed security policies. Your organization should have document security policies in place, too.

The Office of Management and Budget's Cost Principles

The Office of Management and Budget (OMB), an executive office under the president of the United States, releases documents it calls "circulars," or memoranda, about how funds should be managed, especially in regard to federal funds and grants. Even if you've never written a federal grant, you should know that the GPC exam covers all aspects of the grant profession, including the alphabet soup of acronyms cooked up by federal and state agencies. Examples include:

◆ OMB Circular A-21, Cost Principles for Educational Institutions 2 CFR, Part 220

◆ OMB Circular A-87, Cost Principles for State, Local, and Indian Tribal Governments 2 CFR, Part 225

◆ OMB Circular A-122, Cost Principles for Nonprofit Organizations 2 CFR, Part 230

◆ 48 CFR Part 31, For-Profit Organizations

◆ Super Circular! Released on December 26, 2013

   ❖ In 2013, the OMB released its latest grant reform guidelines, frequently referred to as the "Super Circular." The formal name is the "Uniform Administrative Requirements, Cost Principles and Audit Requirements for Federal Awards." This document is available on the OMB website at *http://www.whitehouse.gov/omb/circulars_default*.

   The Super Circular was intended to deliver on the promise of a twenty-first century government that is more efficient, effective, and transparent. The OMB streamlined the federal government's guidance. This guidance provides a government-wide framework for grant management that will be complemented by additional efforts to strengthen program outcomes through innovative and effective use of grantmaking models, performance metrics, and evaluation. The Super Circular rules and regulations went into effect in December 2014 and the OMB guidance is making the work of a grant professional more efficient. This is a good thing!

   ❖ Federal agencies had one year to review the guidance, submit their implementation regulations to the OMB, and establish implementation guidance for their grantees.

◆ 2 CFR Parts 215 and 220, effective December 26, 2014.

The DATA Act 2014

Grant professionals need to know about the Digital Accountability and Transparency Act, or DATA Act. As the acronym implies, the act is about data and government spending data.

The DATA Act makes spending data available to the public at the website *USASpending.gov.* The bill's goal, to quote the Congressional Research Service's (CRS) summary, is to "provide consistent, reliable, and searchable government-wide spending data." That data will "improve the quality of data submitted to *USASpending.gov* by holding federal agencies accountable for the completeness and accuracy of the data submitted," according to the CRS.

> ### Super Circular! 2 CFR Parts 215 and 220
>
> This OMB final guidance supersedes and streamlines requirements from OMB Circulars A-21, A-87, A-110, and A-122 (which have been placed in OMB guidance); Circulars A-89, A-102, and A-133; and the guidance in Circular A-50 on Single Audit Act follow-up.
>
>

The website serves at least two purposes for grant professionals. If you have an active federal award, it's your responsibility to make sure it's listed properly on the website. Also, the website is a terrific resource for information about grants and government spending in general. You can look up your competition and you can sort geographically—even by funding source.

Key Functions of Grant Management

Successful grant procurement can sometimes involve a bit of good luck. However, if there's any area of the grant profession where it is better to be good rather than lucky, it's grant management.

Sound grant management means good monitoring reports and clean audits. Sound grant management comes from good training, thoughtful staff, and the ability to read and follow instructions. Yes, grant professionals should know enough about grant management to craft grant proposals that have taken into account the project milestones, expected outcomes, and reporting requirements. But the greatest results of sound grant management are goods and services delivered efficiently to people in need and the opportunity to apply to the same funder again in the future.

Project implementation is a skill and takes a great deal of effort. Grant management is also a skill. Continued funding relies upon both skills!

Grant management has rules, regulations, and best practices. So, good grant management can also be referred to as "precise" project management!

The key functions of grant management are:

- ◆ Budget development/management
- ◆ Financial tracking
- ◆ Project implementation
- ◆ Monitoring and oversight
- ◆ Reporting and closeout

Budget Development

We often hear supervisors asking program staff if their grant-funded project is "under budget and on time." Program staff often figuratively look (and sometimes literally, during meetings!) to grant staff for the answers. We recommend that this type of information be shared at regular program/grant meetings. Program staff should be able to, at the least, estimate spending levels.

Budget Management

Budget management is a function of grant management. There's no substitute for knowing your grant project's expenditure and revenue budget by heart (preferably in real time).

Financial Tracking

This function involves more than simply generating a project number report from the financial management system (FMS). You may have to compare FMS reports against their own tracking of expenses and help finance staff make adjusted entries (that is, journal entries) to correct these reports. You can help by doing the research and providing the back-up documentation needed by the accounting staff.

Financial tracking is also about proper documentation for expenditures. The level of documentation must be sufficient enough to pass an external audit review, known as "three-way-match documentation." Three-way match refers to these three documents:

1. the vendor's invoice that was received and will become part of an organization's accounts payable record, if approved for payment

2. a purchase order or requisition prepared by the organization

3. the receiving report that was prepared by the organization (the organization may allow the vendor contract/agreement to be used in place of the receiving report)

> ### Cost Principles—"The Rules"
>
> All expenditures related to grants must be necessary, reasonable, allowable, and consistent.
>
> ◆ *Necessary* means that the expenditure must be necessary to carry out the purpose of the grant.
>
> ◆ *Reasonable* means the expenditure must be what a reasonable (think prudent) person would expect to pay for the goods or services.
>
> ◆ *Allowable* means the expenditure must be authorized under the grant and in conformance with the cost principles and not prohibited by federal, state, or local law.
>
> ◆ *Consistent* means the expenditure must be consistent with how other expenditures are made by the grant recipient.
>
>
> important

The three-way match is a review of the invoice, purchase order, and receiving report before the check is cut. Obviously, the amount, number of units, and items purchased must match on all three documents!

Time and Effort for Personnel

Time and effort for personnel is a specific type of documentation to document salary and fringe benefits charges for grant-funded projects. The highest level of documentation to substantiate "time on project" is a separate time sheet pertaining to only the grant project work. The next level is another column on the employee's regular timesheet just for the grant-related activity. A pure percentage of an employee's time on the grant activity is not considered an appropriate level of documentation.

Inventory Controls

Inventory controls are not documentation per se, but rather procedures to guide how the items purchased are maintained and accounted for on the organization's fixed assets' inventory. You should inventory grant-funded assets just like all other fixed assets. The same goes for disposal of grant-funded items. Items purchased with grant dollars should follow the same "surplus" disposal procedures you follow for any other inventory items.

In-kind/Match

In-kind or match requires documentation for the file. In-kind match is not cash, but rather a valuation of funds spent on behalf of the grant project by the organization. In many cases, overhead or indirect costs will be contributed as an in-kind match. Local match, on the other hand, is cash from the organization's own funds (the source is not federal or state funds) used in conjunction with the grant funds to implement the project.

Project Implementation

Project implementation is a skill, much like grant project development is a skill. Grant project implementation involves many moving parts. We recommend starting with the desired outcomes and planning in reverse to meet the "drop-dead" deadlines and self-imposed intermediate deadlines. Although the responsibility for project management often falls on the shoulders of program staff, grant-funded projects should not be burdensome for program staff. Whether the projects they are implementing are grant-funded or not, the project implementation process should be basically the same.

Prior Approval Requirements for Changes

In many cases, prior approval requirements for changes aren't mandatory. But any programmatic change gives you a great chance to communicate with the funder between formal reports. Asking for prior approval shows the funder that you are a good steward of grant dollars. It's worth paying attention to your organization's internal procedures for project changes, especially "in-the-field change orders" that may require prior approval by the funding source. You may need prior authorization to get reimbursed for project-related expenses.

Contractual Services Policies and Procedures

You and your program staff should know and follow your organization's contracting policies and purchasing guidelines. Your organizational guidelines should stipulate how long RFPs/ RFQs are advertised, bid specifications, formal and informal bid processes, conflicts of interest, insurance and performance bond requirements, and any required approval processes. Generally speaking, try to follow the most restrictive policies and guidelines in order to protect the organization and properly steward the grant funds. Short cuts in following contracting rules must be avoided, or else!

Is There a Hierarchy of Rules and Regulations?

Yes! Surprising, isn't it? (Said no seasoned grant professional ever!) The hierarchy of rules and regulations that govern a federal grant is as follows (with 1 being the most important):

1. Program legislation and statutes

2. Program regulations

3. Administrative regulations

4. OMB circulars

5. Grant-award terms and conditions

6. Federal agency policy directives

practical tip

Monitoring and Oversight

Monitoring and oversight are the responsibility of both program and grant staff. Program staff should be prepared for the funding source to make an announced or unannounced site visit to review the grant. The funder source may review grant files, meet with beneficiaries, and interview finance staff about the use of grant funds and if outcomes are being measured. The grant staff are often charged with providing oversight and evaluating the grant project.

Reporting

Reporting is a primary function of grant management that most grant professionals are concerned with on a daily basis. Grant reporting requirements are as varied as the number and type of grants that exist. Many larger foundations require online grant reporting through web portals. Some reports are paper-based and must be signed in blue ink by an authorized official and sent via the US mail. Other funders request reports by email with attachments describing activities, including media coverage, and/or photos.

Grant Managers Unite!

Grant management must follow sound business practices. For example:

◆ Arm's length bargaining (that is, procurement processes)

◆ Compliance with federal, state, and local laws

◆ Compliance with the terms of the grant award

◆ Adherence to fair market prices and no significant deviation from established prices

◆ Deliberate decisions and prudent action

important

Funders typically set report deadlines in a grant contract, grant agreement, or award letter. These deadlines can be monthly, quarterly, or annual. Contact the funder as soon as possible if you have any questions about the format or deadline. The mark of a successful grant management expert is that all grant reports are turned in on time, or early!

Closeout

Closeout is the most rewarding function of grant management! The closeout process includes preparing and submitting any final report to the funder as well as preparing the content used in annual reports and program evaluation summaries. No discussion of closeout procedures would be complete without mentioning the end-of-year audit, which takes place after the funds have been spent AND reimbursed. This process can take months and can span more than one fiscal year. The audit may take six months or more to publish after the fiscal year ends. In fact, the closeout process may take longer than it took to spend the grant funds. Audits are important but often not required for all grant projects. Some funding sources require that the organizational audit be submitted to them for review. The funding source, based on its review of the audit, may require additional procedures and/or internal controls to be implemented by the grantee.

Record Maintenance and Retention

Record maintenance and retention are vital to any grant management operation. Some grant-related documents are considered "permanent records" and must be maintained by the organization. Make sure to follow your state's record retention policy, including the timely destruction of grant records not considered permanent.

Depending on the size of your organization, each grant management role and responsibility may be handled by a separate job or an entire department. For start-ups and other small nonprofits, you may need an industrial-strength hat rack to provide enough storage space for all the hats each staffer may need to wear daily. Large, medium, or small organizations all need the same types of functions for successful grant management. The scale and scope are the only differences.

Roles and Responsibilities

Having proper internal controls also means establishing specific roles and responsibilities for project, management, and other key staff. In an ideal world, all of this information would be magically updated and stored each quarter in a secure online file. Then all you'd need to do is to simply download and print, or attach it to an online proposal. All your problems would be solved, and tiny bluebirds of happiness would nest in your office. If this is your situation, congratulations— we're jealous! But for the rest of us, establishing, or at least clarifying in writing, the roles and responsibilities of staff members as they relate to grants falls within the grant professional's job.

Cross-training is important when folks are out on vacation or medical leave, or away from their computers. The grant professional's role in grant management is to implement the project in a manner that does the most good. Although every project is different, these duties are often covered by the "other duties as assigned" statement on your job description!

It would seem that everyone in your organization has a role in grants, administration, and closeout. Let's look closer. A description of duties and responsibilities is a good place for us to start.

Chief Elected Official

In governmental agencies, the chief elected official is the person responsible for committing or obligating the organization. A grant agreement obligates organizational resources, especially financial resources such as matching funds, and programmatic resources such as staff. The chief elected official is often the head of a political body and makes sure that appropriate policies are upheld and implemented. The mayor (for municipalities), commission chair (for counties, regional bodies, and quasigovernmental agencies), and the governor (for states) are authorized to sign grant applications and grant agreements. The chief elected official can designate persons to sign in their absence. For example, a mayor pro tem can sign grant documents when a mayor is on vacation.

Grant Management Has a Goal?

Grant management isn't just a phrase or title. Shocking, isn't it? The goals of grant management are to:

◆ Implement the grant project

◆ Follow the rules

◆ Benefit the greatest number of people (or animals)

◆ Document the results

◆ Report the outcomes

important

Chief Executive Officer

In governmental agencies, the chief executive officer, or CEO, can also obligate the organization. The city manager, county manager, or state-level department head are often authorized signatories for grants. The CEO is responsible for managing the day-to-day operations of the agency and reports directly to a city council or board of commissioners.

In nonprofits, the CEO is the person most frequently authorized to sign grant applications. The organization's managing director or chief executive is responsible for managing the organization. The CEO is usually the most senior executive or administrator. This person typically reports directly to a board of directors. The CEO can designate others, such as department heads or attorneys, to sign grant documents in the CEO's absence.

Finance Director

The finance director (often called chief financial officer or CFO) oversees the finances of an organization, business, institution, or agency. The CFO's job is to make sure that the finances are kept in order and to communicate information about financial issues to other members of the organization and, sometimes, to the general public and/or stockholders. The finance director is ultimately responsible for the organization's finances and procuring the audit. Ideally, the grant staff works closely with the finance director and finance staff.

Grant Accounting Personnel

Grant accounting personnel are responsible for ensuring that timely billings are prepared on cost reimbursement contracts and for requesting funds for grants or contracts. They process all correspondence regarding business, financial, and administrative matters and act as a liaison with sponsors.

Grant Manager or Grant Administrator (Preaward)

Grant managers work with internal staff to determine funding needs and how funds are being, and will be, used. They also work with external organizations such as foundations and governmental agencies to acquire funding. A grant manager is responsible for all grants managed by the organization. The grant manager is responsible for the day-to-day operations of the grant-seeking and grant administration functions of the organization.

The job requires strong writing skills, since most grant applications require in-depth descriptions (including the proposed use of the funds). This position also requires strong accounting and finance skills, since a grant manager at a nonprofit may also have to handle internal auditing and bookkeeping to ensure grant money is properly spent. At an academic institution or larger nonprofit, these roles may be split between separate finance and preaward or proposal development personnel. At a smaller nonprofit, these functions are generally merged into a single grant manager role.

A grant manager generally works entirely in an office setting and rarely travels to a granting institution to deliver a proposal. Usually, the grant manager works with the organization's internal team and delivers the proposal via mail or email to the funder. These professionals typically work during regular business hours, although overtime might be required, especially as deadlines approach. Previous experience in grants and grant writing is generally needed as well. In addition to strong writing, accounting, and finance skills, grant managers should be excellent communicators who work well under deadlines.

Grant Coordinator or Grant Specialist

The grant coordinator or grant specialist is a position that can be either preaward or postaward. The position usually works with internal staff to develop and/or submit grant applications or with external partners to implement grant awards. Both positions are very versatile and require deep grants knowledge and familiarity with a variety of grant programs.

The job requires strong writing skills, sound financial accounting, and bookkeeping skills. Previous experience in grant implementation and grant writing is generally needed as well.

A grant coordinator generally works with a number of different grants. The coordinator position manages many grant projects at once. A grants specialist works with a specific grant or on all grants the organization receives from a particular grantmaking entity. The specialist is familiar with all of the rules and regulations pertaining to grant administration and project implementation.

Grant Project Administrator/Director (Postaward)

A grant administrator is in charge of appropriating grants within an organization such as a foundation. This person processes the paperwork and applications, gives out the grants, and ensures that the funds are spent according to specified terms. Grant administrators will often deal with five or more grantees at a time, keeping track of details and distributing funds as appropriate for each one. Most grant administrators handle budgets for clients that range from $2 million to $5 million.

If you're thinking of working in this field, there is no specific set of courses to take. A bachelor's degree is often required. You might think about taking research-related coursework or choosing a major that involves research. Having this background would be helpful, because research is involved in many grant programs. After receiving a bachelor's degree, become certified in grant management. Seminars are offered by groups such as the National Grants Management Association (NGMA). Grant administrators can take training in one of three different tracks within grant management: federal track, pass-through track, or recipient track.

Program Director and Program Staff

A program director is a person who develops or selects some or all of the activities or services delivered to clients. The program director and associated staff play a key role in grant management as they are on the front lines, delivering services to people and carrying out the mission of the organization. The program director is responsible for collecting client data, reporting out accomplishments, spending grant funds, notifying grant staff of issues, and implementing the grant.

Internal Auditor

An independent financial professional performs work for an organization but is not employed by it. An internal auditor, on the other hand, works for the organization being reviewed. Both parties provide similar services, including the evaluation of financial statements, business operations, and compliance with regional rules as well as offering their opinions on efficiency and finding possible fraud. Internal examiners generally have the advantage when it comes to understanding industry- or company-specific characteristics, but knowing the people being audited can interfere with their judgment.

An internal auditor works with the grant and program staff to ensure that the grant project is being implemented correctly. The internal auditor can identify problems early and work with the organization's staff to correct issues before the monitoring or end-of-the-year audit. The internal auditor is an important collaborator with staff in the grant management process.

Funder's Program Officer

Funders, or grantmakers, hire program officers to assist in the implementation of programs. For example, program officers may assist grantees in implementing grant-funded projects that promote postsecondary access and success for low-income, first-generation and underrepresented students. The program officer may support pathways for students or build the capacity of institutions that focus on low-income and underrepresented students. The program officer is typically part of a team that works with domestic programs. However, this person may also oversee an international program that supports postsecondary access and success, for example.

Program officers manage grantmaking activities for foundations and organizations. These officers use a full array of tools available to foster change. These tools include planning grants, project grants, and general operating support. They may deal with program-related investments for organizations whose work directly corresponds with funding priorities. Program officers work in close partnership with program staff, grant management staff, and peer foundations.

External Auditor

Every grant the organization administers will be accounted for in the annual audit of financial statements. External auditors are either paid by an organization or come from an outside entity.

An external auditor is a third-party professional who performs an independent review of an organization's financial records. These individuals are often CPAs. An external auditor evaluates accounting, payroll, and purchasing records, as well as anything related to financial investments and loans, searching for any mistakes or fraud. Afterwards, the external auditor provides an accurate, unbiased report to management. External and internal auditors typically perform similar work, although an internal review is generally more focused on risk management and internal control procedures.

The grant monitor is an employee of the grantmaking entity who is responsible for reviewing the grantee's files, systems, and grant projects to make sure the rules are followed. The grant monitoring may also be called the "final inspection." It's the final step in the grant management process. After the final inspection is complete and the report is accepted, the organization is authorized to submit the last request for reimbursement.

Transition to Postaward

A grant award is the first step in the grant postaward process. The next step is usually seeking and obtaining internal approval to accept the funds, setting up the budget within the financial management system, and obligating any matching funds. The postaward process often includes a kick-off meeting with grant, program, and finance staff. Including other stakeholders in the kick-off meetings is recommended. For example, transportation-related grant projects might include police or other public safety personnel, especially if the street needs to be blocked by equipment during construction of waterline mains.

A major function of grant management is completing and submitting required forms and reports. In many cases, submitting these required forms to the funder starts the postaward period, meaning that the costs incurred by the grantee after the postaward period starts can be counted as grant-related expenses.

Desk Audit and Site Visit Monitoring

Grant management often involves participating in desk audits and site visit monitoring. These tasks are very different from preaward site visits. Preaward site visits can be likened to a job interview, whereas postaward site visits are more like personnel evaluations. The purpose of these audits and visits is to ensure the grantee is adhering the the grant or contract requirements and to provide on-site technical assistance. They are also an opportunity for the grantor and grantee to work together as the project progresses. They should never be looked at as punitive.

No-cost Time Extensions

If you need more time to complete the scope of work for a project, you often have the option of requesting a no-cost time extension. The grant period—the start and end dates of the grant—is stipulated in the grant agreement and can only be changed by the funder. You'll need to submit a request in writing to the funder to get your project extended beyond the original end date. The funder may ask you for additional information, including the cause of the delay, before acting on your request. The funder can either say "yes" or "no"—remember, this isn't a done deal!

Closeout Procedures and Audits

Closeout procedures and audits are the ultimate postaward activities. The closeout process cannot begin until all grant expenditures are posted and accounted for in the financial management system. Another often-overlooked component of closeout is the reimbursement process. All grant revenues must be received and accounted for in the financial management system before closing out the grant. This may seem obvious to most, but closing out a grant before receiving the check is a bad idea!

Audits

Audits occur whether or not the funds are spent and received. External auditors perform "tests" of the accounting systems and look for irregularities and deficiencies. Audits occur at regular intervals based on the organization's fiscal year. If the funds have been spent but not reimbursed, the audit findings might suggest to management that the grant program isn't performing as it should. Nonreimbursed funds should be "booked" as a receivable in the financial management system. Grant expenditures, requisitioned but not paid at the end of the fiscal year, should be booked as an "account payable" in the financial management system. Grant and finance staff must be aware of this and be able to explain receivables and payables to auditors.

Effective Grant Development

Grant project design and development is an important skill for grant professionals. As a proposal writer, you should be able to design and write the project well enough for a grant reviewer to assess whether that project can be implemented successfully. Grant proposal reviewers will rely upon their personal and professional experience to evaluate the timeline, costs, equipment needs, regulatory limitations, and budget amounts as proposed before making a recommendation for an award.

An extremely important question on grant applications is, "How will your proposed project be self-sustaining?" The answer should never be, "to seek and obtain more grants." Although this is a tempting answer, it's misleading for a number of reasons.

First and foremost, grants are for new and creative projects. Secondly, grants can be used for general

---

Do You Need Prior Approval?

Now that you have the grant in hand, you can do whatever you want, right? Wrong! You may have changes in your organization, for example, that affect your grant. You need to let the funder know about these changes and sometimes get their approval, particularly if it's a federal grant. If you have a federal grant, you'll need prior approval from the agency to make the following changes:

◆ Change in scope or objective

◆ Change in key personnel

◆ Authority to bring in a third-party contractor

◆ Certain budget transfers (10 percent of total budget rule)

◆ Interruption of the program (for more than three months)

important

operating support and ongoing programs or projects. Rarely, if ever, are grants available for projects the organization is required by law to perform. If the tempting answer to sustaining the program is to write more grants, you've missed the intent of the question. The funding source is asking the question about sustainability to learn about your approach to funding the project without future funding from them. The funder wants to see other partners, an organizational budget plan, program income, a donor plan, or community business sponsors. Take care to establish a sustainability plan that doesn't rely on one type or source of funding.

Secondly, the answer "to seek and obtain more grants" is insulting to the grant reviewer. If the reviewer feels you're devaluing the grant opportunity during the application phase, the reviewer is unlikely to recommend an award. Keep the focus of each grant on the needs and expectations of the grantmaker for the funds and on those you both want to serve. Put yourself in the funder's role and ask yourself what you'd want to see in a proposal that would make you want to fund a project.

Finally, the secret desire of grantmakers is to be a part of something great. They don't want to waste their money on a long shot or a fluke. Your job, as a grant developer, is to use your experience in grant management to wisely and appropriately spend the grant funds.

Internal Approvals and Processes

Grant professionals must know and follow internal financial and programmatic procedures. Your organization should have proper procedures in place for financial processes such as requisitions, payments, accounts receivable, and contingency funds. The same is true for programmatic processes, reporting requirements, and use of data collection systems. Many federal grantmakers host mandatory grant implementation workshops for grant managers, program staff, and accounting folks. The workshops are helpful for both new staff and experienced personnel.

Staffing Resource Considerations

Proper staffing and personnel turnover are important considerations. Internal staff changes can result in numerous challenges for any organization that must be considered. Turnover at the grantmaking or funding source can heavily impact the grant project and could cause unexpected delays. Many federal grantmakers host mandatory grant implementation workshops and training sessions for grant managers, program staff, and accounting folks. Training is a time-consuming but necessary endeavor. Training time should be a factor considered during the grant development phase. The duties may differ for grant projects, but all duties are still covered by "other duties as assigned" on your job description.

Grant Agreement and Special Terms and Conditions

You can find the statutes, regulations, and terms and conditions in the grant award agreement. A typical agreement spells out the grant reporting requirements, how the funder wishes to be acknowledged (in print, electronic media, or not at all), how to use its logo on signage, and contact information for the program officer. Unfortunately, not every grant award has an agreement. In this case, you should follow your organization's standard procedures or industry best practices.

Monitoring and Oversight

Monitoring and oversight consist of four areas:

◆ Performance oversight

◆ Monitoring and analysis

◆ Complaint resolution

◆ Audit and investigations

We Recommend Checks, Cross-checks, and Balances!

Successful grant management can't occur without tracking the awarded funds. You shouldn't rely on your organization's financial management system any more than you would rely upon your bank to track your personal bank account. Always use a spreadsheet to track grant expenditures and revenues, in the same fashion you use a checkbook to track your personal banking activity. Enter each expense, reimbursement submitted, and revenue in chronological order. During the audit, or program monitoring, you'll be glad you did.

 practical tip

Performance oversight involves monitoring electronic and paper data, complaint handling, entity audits, and enforcement actions. Oversight encourages and rewards excellence and continuous improvement. It also fosters improved and timely communications; evaluates performance objectives, outcome measures, and project expectations; and focuses on results.

Complaint resolution seeks to encourage communications and assist in resolving complaints. The complaint-resolution process routinely results in additional participants and documentation for outcomes measurement.

Audits and investigations are compliance investigations and performance audits of grant spending, reporting, and participant activities/beneficiaries. If a complaint is found to be unjustified, no further action is taken. Justified complaints are forwarded for mediation and/or enforcement within the US Code, grant rules, audits, and regulations.

As a grant professional, you should strive to understand contracts and the contracting process within your organization. Your organization's procurement policies and requirements must be followed when spending grant funds. Your procurement policies and requirements should be as restrictive as the federal procurement requirements.

Closeout and Continuation Funding (or Sustainability) Plan

The grant closeout process typically includes a final report to the funder as well as preparing the content used in annual reports. The final report can be a formal written report. More often, however, the final report is an email or letter informing the funder that the project is complete. Many funders appreciate a short report showing the accomplishments of the grant and pictures of the grant activities and people served.

The funder may want to see other partners, an organizational budget plan, program income, a donor plan, or community business sponsors. Make sure that your organization doesn't rely too heavily on grants, but instead uses a balanced approach.

Continuation funding is more often than not the result of good grant management. Approval of a grant project often includes support for a project period spanning several years. An award of funding, however, is generally made on an annual basis, subject to the availability of funds and evidence of the project's ongoing progress. Annual progress reports are considered as evidence of the success or failure of a grant project. Typically, the initial award provides funds for the first twelve-month period of the project and indicates the support recommended for each budget period within the remainder of the project period. Continuation funding for future years often hinges upon the grant reports submitted to the funder.

Even though it may sometimes feel like you're treading water in a sea of alphabet soup filled with government and private acronyms, forms, circulars, and other regulatory documents, sound grant management is vitally important! Without it, your organization will find it nearly impossible to secure continued funding. More importantly, the communities you serve will suffer if your organization can't or won't provide follow-through in postaward grant management.

Are You Exam Ready?

You are exam ready if you can:

- Identify standard elements of regulatory compliance

- Identify effective practices for key functions of grant management

- Differentiate roles and responsibilities of project and management staff and other key principals affiliated with grant projects

- Identify methods of establishing transitions to postaward implementation that fulfill project applications

Chapter Six

Ethics

IN THIS CHAPTER

···→ What is the GPA Code of Ethics?

···→ Why is ethical behavior important?

···→ How do I recognize ethical threats?

···→ How do I resolve ethical dilemmas?

This chapter covers GPCI Competency Six: "Knowledge of nationally-recognized standards of ethical practices by grant professionals." This competency represents 10 percent of the multiple-choice exam questions.

Eth • i • cal: Seven letters rich in meaning, strong in power. We are drawn to ethical professionals because they create an environment of safety and trust.

A strong ethical framework upholds GPCI's and GPA's vision, mission, and values statements and their ethical codes. In fact, in order to be a member of GPA or to sit for the certification exam, you must agree to follow GPA's code of professional conduct, referred to as the GPA Code of Ethics.

In news stories of misspending restricted grant funds on luxury cars, exotic travel, or phantom real estate deals, obvious unethical behavior stands out on page or screen. But not all choices facing grant professionals are so clear-cut. In fact, most aren't.

This chapter discusses the importance of a strong ethical framework through the use of examples and scenarios. We'll explore the differences between the "letter of the law" and the "spirit of obligation," and what it means to be a responsible grant professional.

By the way, the fact that you're reading this chapter speaks to your desire to advance the field and to your commitment to protect the entities you serve. The point is not to memorize everything in this chapter, but to use it as a springboard to think critically about this important topic.

The Meaning of Ethics in Its Most Basic Form

According to Merriam-Webster, *ethics* is defined as "a)… the principles of conduct governing an individual or group; b) a guiding philosophy." Ethics are guidelines, not legal mandates; values, not binding contracts.

In fact, according to the Puget Sound Grantwriters Association, being ethical in grant writing means to "… be honest, tell the truth, the whole truth, and nothing but the truth. This applies to both narratives and budgets." Easy, right?

The tricky part is that most ethical challenges happen when we don't realize that our actions are pushing professional boundaries. Maybe you haven't recognized any ethical conflicts in your work, and you might question the necessity of devoting any more than a cursory look at this issue. But reviewing and internalizing the GPA Code of Ethics can provide a solid foundation for any grant professional.

The Letter and Spirit of the GPA Code of Ethics

The term "letter of the law" is often regarded as close adherence to a law, mandate, contract, or agreement. The "spirit of the law" speaks to the individual's belief in the value of the law. People obey laws (most of the time) but their acceptance of the law—or code of ethics—may be filtered through a lens of "how the law affects *me*," and what are the outcomes "if *I* break the law."

The spirit of the law asks you to take a step back from the written words of the law and to understand, and ultimately internalize, the principles guiding the law. You'll be looking at the law through the lens of how the law benefits, rather than restricts, the community and its culture.

To get at the core of the spirit of the law, we must appreciate why the law is important. To understand the spirit of *ethics* in the grant profession, we need to recognize how a shared ethical framework operates in tandem to grow and professionalize the field, and protect those who rely on us for their own growth and development.

The Importance of Ethics—the Potential for Abuse

Every year, more than $350 billion changes hands in some form of charitable dollars for goods and services in the United States. An estimated one hundred thousand individuals serve as grant professionals for funders and organizations seeking grant funding.

To date, the law does not require grant professionals to have special training, education, or license to practice grantsmanship such as is required for, say, lawyers and doctors. Yet, we're part of a profession, and are expected by our peers to understand and conform to our profession's ethical standards. When we seek recognition of our hard-won expertise by working toward professional certification, it's our peers who are providing the certification—not the government.

To many in the nonprofit sector, grant writing is viewed as a technical skill easily acquired with a few days of training. Administrators may not know that it is unethical to hire a grant developer for a percentage of the grant award. Midnight infomercials claim that government grants are "free money," training programs promise professional certification in a week, and grant consultants advertise 100 percent success rates to unsuspecting nonprofits.

Consequently, too many nonprofits spend precious dollars unsuccessfully seeking funds and funders receive proposals with little chance for success. It's no surprise that certain actors in the grant profession have come under fire, along with others engaged in fundraising. In the past few years, several states have instituted fundraiser registration requirements.

Uneducated nonprofits and the absence of formal education and regulation in the grant field create opportunity for abuse and unethical practice. This hurts the nonprofits, of course. It also hurts the grant profession. Most importantly, it hurts the communities that stand to benefit from grant funding.

GPCI believes it's essential for the nonprofit community, as well as the community-at-large, to understand the role grant professionals play in the overall health of a nonprofit organization and the power they have over fund-seeking outcomes. As a grant professional, you have an *ethical obligation* to strengthen the nonprofit community's ability to guide and shape the outcomes of its funding endeavors through education.

> ### Nonprofits Everywhere!
>
> More than 1.5 million nonprofits or charitable organizations are on file with the IRS as of the writing of this book. That's a lot of competition!
>
> **observation**

GPA Code of Ethics—the Fundamentals

The GPA Code of Ethics is based on the AFP Code of Ethical Principles and Standards of Professional Practice. In fact, in 1997 GPA obtained permission to adopt the AFP code and publically acknowledge AFP in its contribution to GPA's Code of Ethics. This was a very ethical way to go about it!

> ### Community Ethics Education
>
> In your grant arsenal, you need to have the tools to educate the nonprofit community about grant-related ethical practices. It's up to the profession to educate nonprofit leaders about our field.
>
> **practical tip**

GPA's Code of Ethics undergoes ongoing review and revision as determined by the membership. The last revision was in October 2011. While long in words and wide-ranging in concept, it serves as the foundation of the grant profession. It is included in this chapter in its entirety. This is where we must begin. When you come out on "the other side" after reading this important information, we'll take a look at what it means to and for us. See you there!

If you've never read the GPA Code of Ethics, or haven't read them lately, we recommend doing so now. Instead of burying them in an index at the end of this manual, we're making them front and center, right here in this chapter, in the different font. So, go ahead. Read them. We'll wait.

GPA Members, among others, are to:

◆ Practice their profession with the highest sense of integrity, honesty, and truthfulness to maintain and broaden public confidence.

◆ Adhere to all applicable laws and regulations in all aspects of grantsmanship.

◆ Continually improve their professional knowledge and skills.

◆ Promote positive relationships between grant professionals and their stakeholders.

> ### American Association of Grant Professionals
>
> One driving force that led to the formation of AAGP was the erosion of grant ethics. A second concern was a perceived need for a professional credential. AAGP changed its name to the Grant Professionals Association in 2010.
>
> **observation**

◆ Value the privacy, freedom, choice and interests of all those affected by their actions.

◆ Ensure that funds are solicited according to program guidelines.

◆ Adhere to acceptable means of compensation for services performed; pro bono work is encouraged.

◆ Foster cultural diversity and pluralistic values and treat all people with dignity and respect.

◆ Become leaders and role models in the field of grantsmanship.

◆ Encourage colleagues to embrace and practice GPA's Code of Ethics and Standards of Professional Practice.

Standards of Professional Practice

As members respect and honor the above principles and guidelines established by the GPA Code of Ethics, any infringement or breach of standards outlined in the code are subject to disciplinary sanctions, including expulsion, to be determined by a committee elected by their peers.

Professional Obligations:

1. Members shall act according to the highest ethical standards of their institution, profession, and conscience.

2. Members shall obey all applicable local, state, provincial, and federal civil and criminal laws and regulations.

3. Members shall avoid the appearance of any criminal offense or professional misconduct.

4. Members shall disclose all relationships that might constitute, or appear to constitute, conflicts of interest.

5. Members shall not be associated directly or indirectly with any service, product, individuals, or organizations in a way that they know is misleading.

6. Members shall not abuse any relationship with a donor, prospect, volunteer or employee to the benefit of the member or the member's organization.

7. Members shall recognize their individual boundaries of competence and are forthcoming and truthful about their professional experience, knowledge and expertise.

8. Members shall continually strive to improve their personal competence.

Solicitation and Use of Funds:

9. Members shall take care to ensure that all solicitation materials are accurate and correctly reflect the organization's mission and use of solicited funds.

10. Members shall take care to ensure that grants are used in accordance with the grant's intent.

If Applicable:

11. Members shall take care to ensure proper use of funds, including timely reports on the use and management of such funds.

12. Members shall obtain explicit consent by the grantor before altering the conditions of grant agreements.

Presentation of Information:

13. Members shall not disclose privileged information to unauthorized parties. Information acquired from consumers is confidential. This includes verbal and written disclosures, records, and video or audio recording of an activity or presentation without appropriate releases.

14. Members shall not plagiarize in any professional work, including, but not limited to: grant proposals, journal articles/magazines, scholarly works, advertising/marketing materials, websites, scientific articles, self-plagiarism, etc.

15. Members are responsible for knowing the confidentiality regulations within their jurisdiction.

16. Members shall use accurate and consistent accounting methods that conform to the appropriate guidelines adopted by the American Institute of Certified Public Accountants (AICPA) for the type of organization involved. (In countries outside of the United States, comparable authority should be utilized.)

Compensation:

17. Members shall work for a salary or fee.

18. Members may accept performance-based compensation, such as bonuses, provided such bonuses are in accordance with prevailing practices within the members' own organizations and are not based on a percentage of grant monies.

19. Members shall not accept or pay a finder's fee, commission, or percentage compensation based on grants and shall take care to discourage their organizations from making such payments.

20. Compensation should not be written into grants unless allowed by the funder."

Connecting the Dots between Action and Outcome

Grant-related ethical challenges take many forms. This section reviews some of the ethical challenges we face every day as grant professionals.

Google "grant ethics" and nearly 100 percent of all queries will lead you to one topic: commission-based compensation, also referred to as the dreaded CBC by this manual's authors. It's the most popular topic regarding ethical dilemmas in the grant field.

Commission-based Compensation

Commission-based compensation (CBC) most commonly occurs when someone writes a grant with the understanding that payment will come as a percentage of the award or a bonus fee if the grant is awarded. The concept of bonus creates its share of ethical confusion. Receiving a bonus is an accepted business practice for recognizing a job well done. But when does receiving a bonus become ethically problematic? A breach occurs when the two parties negotiate *only* a bonus if a grant application is funded.

While not illegal, this type of compensation violates the GPA Code of Ethics. Here are some of the key reasons why:

◆ With rare exception, government funders and many private funders expressly forbid any grant funds to be used for the preparation of the grant application. Ignorance of this prohibition is no excuse.

◆ The amount of work required to develop a grant may not accurately tie to the final amount awarded and doesn't necessarily relate to the level of expertise of the grant professional.

◆   CBC may place undue emphasis on grants for organizations that may not be able to manage grants.

There are two primary scenarios when grant professionals are not paid for their grant work: the grant was not funded, or the work was done pro bono with no expectation of payment. Some professionals believe that an ethical breach occurs when grant professionals work pro bono. This belief is incorrect. Pro bono work is ethical, encouraged, and respected.

Many CBC discussions center on the losses incurred by a grant professional. They often focus on how much free content is given away to nonprofits for their use in the future. Very little is said about the risks facing the grant professional who engages in CBC. Here, risk often falls into two central categories: submitting a poorly-crafted application due to grant professional inexperience, or submitting a well-crafted application whose program goals cannot be successfully achieved—submitted due to the grant professional's inexperience or need to pay the rent. Clearly, there are no winners in these scenarios. CBC is not to anyone's advantage.

A well-thought-out program plan is key to any successful grant application. It puts forth strategies that the nonprofit can realistically and successfully carry out, designed around the nonprofit's infrastructure and assets. Those of us with longevity in the field know that funders "talk." They lament with their colleagues about the off-the-point, off-mission, and off-the-wall applications they receive. And they recall these nonprofits by name and how often they submit. Over time, a grant-seeking organization gets labeled before its application is even read. So there's no real advantage to using CBC with the organization, either. Saving a few bucks by paying a grant writer a percentage of the award does no good if the organization gets a bad reputation and doesn't get funded. Everyone loses.

Less Pronounced but Equally Significant Ethical Challenges

Not all situations are as obvious as commission-based grant work. Consider the following ethical challenges.

Plagiarism

Plagiarism in the grant profession may not take the traditional form of taking credit for the written work of others without attribution. The challenge to the ethical grant professional is often in less obvious ways, like when need statements aren't properly documented. Even though grant applications aren't considered published material in a traditional sense, a grant review committee can and will ask for back-up documentation on research studies cited.

> ### Plagiarize, Finder's Fee, and Commission
>
> *Plagiarize*—to steal or use the work of another as your own. This can be words, ideas, or entire passages.
>
> *Finder's fee*—payment made for introducing a nonprofit to a funder and/or contingent upon the nonprofit receiving a grant from that funder.
>
> *Commission*—flat-rate fee or percentage paid for services rendered when a grant is awarded.
>
>

Character limits often keep full citations from the final application, understandably. But be sure to keep a list of what you cited on file not only for the current pending grant, but for future grants as well. Consultants who may submit grants to the same funder on behalf of different clients must exercise special caution to keep from plagiarizing themselves! A review committee will certainly realize that they're reading the same version with slight variations. This jeopardizes funding for all those organizations that are victims of a cut-and-paste job.

An important tool used to advance a profession is the publication of scholarly or field-based work. Since the founding of GPA, grant professionals have been actively engaged in this genre by contributing written work to the *JGPA* and via presentations on research and professional practice at conferences. We encourage every experienced grant professional to consider contributing to our professional body of knowledge. You must be careful not to plagiarize work in journal articles, online blog posts, or in presentations. Conducting yourself in an ethical manner goes well beyond writing and submitting proposals.

Historically, grant professionals have entered the field through the door of social justice or human services rather than through research-based academia. While many of us hold advanced academic degrees, our knowledge of plagiarism and what constitutes plagiarism may be limited. It's not surprising that we sometimes see grant professionals called out for plagiarism, and that in most cases the offender had no idea that an ethical breech had been committed.

We often worry about inadvertent plagiarism in our own work and find the following checklist helpful. We hope you do too.

According to *plagiarism.org,* "all of the following are considered plagiarism:

◆ turning in someone else's work as your own

◆ copying words or ideas from someone else without giving credit

◆ failing to put a quotation in quotation marks

◆ giving incorrect information about the source of a quotation

◆ changing words but copying the sentence structure of a source without giving credit

◆ copying so many words or ideas from a source that it makes up the majority of your work, whether you give credit or not (see our section on 'fair use' rules)."

(Reprinted with, of course, permission of *plagiarism. org,* a free resource sponsored by iParadigms LLC.)

Confidentiality

The GPA Code of Ethics states that: "Members shall not disclose privileged information to unauthorized parties. Information acquired from consumers is confidential."

Grant professionals are often privy to the inner workings of the organization they're working for. This information may include top-level salaries, past

---

Need More on Plagiarism?

Learn more about plagiarism at *plagiarism.org.* A little prevention is well worth your while.

Check Up on Us

Did you ask yourself if it's okay that we included the *plagiarism.org* information in this book? Let's see. Here's what the *plagiarism.org* website states on the footer of every page: "In the interest of disseminating this information as widely as possible, *plagiarism.org* grants all reprint and usage requests without the need to obtain any further permission as long as the URL of the original article/information is cited."

So far, so good.

Example

mistakes, and plans for the future. Funders routinely request this information for grant applications. But disclosure of such information to others without the permission of the organization is a clear breach of confidentiality. We also know that we really should not disclose the names of our clients and their grant application histories. So, when does this seemingly black-and-white ethical consideration become grey? Connections can be made more intuitively.

> ### What about Making Stuff Up?
>
> Do not engage in any grant activity that causes you to "make stuff up." Not only is it unethical, it will eventually lead to a bad reputation for you and your organization.
>
>

Show Me the Money

The phrase "show me the money" was popularized in the 1996 film *Jerry Maguire*. In the grant field, it represents the missteps made by nonprofits that chase funding without thinking about their organization's vision, mission, and values. Sometimes this is done with blatant disregard. Other times it occurs because a potential conflict between the funder and the organization's mission isn't readily identified. More often, though, it occurs because neither the organization nor the grant professional has ever engaged in a broad-based critical discussion about a potential conflict of interest. In other words, it has never occurred to either stakeholder that a funder's history could be problematic.

Chasing Dollars—Mission Drift

Mission drift occurs when an organization begins programs, services, or other activities that are inconsistent with its intended mission and strategic plans. Mission drift occurs for many reasons. There could be a change in a board or executive leadership, or a lack of understanding of the relationship between mission and activity. The organizational leadership could see a potential funding opportunity that may not fit. Or there may be a grant professional who doesn't fully understand the entity's mission. The organization's stakeholders could also be unaware or inexperienced as to the implications of mission drift. Below is one example of how a grant seeker may be tempted by mission drift.

When organizations are desperate for funding, they risk applying for grant dollars that move them away from their mission or charter. This can be time wasted on unrealistic grant proposals that could be better spent in other fundraising activities. Or, if the mission-drift proposal gets funded, the organization may have to divert staff and funding from existing programs. This can lead to a cycle of short-lived projects with poor or nonexistent programs—not a healthy, sustainable program that offers long-term benefits for those it serves.

As grant professionals, we have an ethical responsibility to look out for mission drift, and when we see it, to inform and educate.

Be aware that a responsible organization engages in strategic planning every three to five years. This usually involves board, staff, and sometimes external consultants. In fact, many foundations require a copy of the current strategic plan as part of standard attachments for a grant application. This isn't mission drift; it's good strategic planning.

Working with Competing Entities for the Same Grant

As mentioned before, many grant consultants develop grants for different organizations that are competing for the same grant initiative. On the one hand, they may represent to their clients—in good faith—that they are objective and committed to the act of writing a compelling grant that is very specific to the strengths of each organization. On the other hand, they may also disclose, in their standard written disclosures, that they may be submitting multiple grants from different clients to the same funder.

Here's a scenario to ponder as an ethical grant professional. Suppose a grant consultant discloses to a potential client that the consulting is already working on an application for another other organization in response to the same RFP. Understandably, the potential client asks for the name of the other organization. Will the grant professional breach confidentiality and disclose the name of the other organization?

Beyond this potential breach is the question of grant-seeker vulnerability. Does the nonprofit have adequate knowledge to grasp the potential conflict of interest being posed by the grant professional?

Finally, suppose that the potential client signs on to become the consultant's client. What happens if one of the consultant's other clients wins the grant, but not the client at hand?

The Last-minute Grant

If you've been in the grant profession for any length of time, you've been faced with the dreaded last-minute grant. With so little time, data and other facts may not be fully vetted. Budgets and program plans are thrown together with best guesstimates, as you work desperately at 3 a.m. Can't lie, we've all been there. Keeping current outcomes and other data on your organization's programs and activities will go a long way to minimize last-minute madness and will prevent you from misrepresenting information.

The Numbers Game

In 1954, Darrell Huff coined the phrase "lying with statistics." He described the power of charts and graphs and how easily they can be manipulated either innocently or with the goal to deceive.

> ### Who's Responsible for Ethical Guidance?
>
> It's *your* ethical obligation to guide an entity away from bad grant-seeking behaviors.
>
> **principle**

> ### Use Statistics Wisely!
>
> Transparency and honesty in budgets and statistics are key elements of ethical practice. Applying grades K-5 data in a preschool grant application to illustrate need raises an ethical red flag.
>
>
> **!**
> important

We use them to help the reader understand our message. In our zeal, we craft them to illustrate the strongest picture possible. And in the process, we may inadvertently distort our numbers, sometimes by blending relevant with less-relevant data. Be careful of committing an ethical error here. You don't want to intentionally deceive with a numbers game.

Today's grant reviewers are savvy about budgets and statistics. They often give special scrutiny to these areas, particularly when they don't have strong content knowledge in the topic area.

Differing Points of View and Their Impact on Ethics

Our profession is experiencing a shift in its public face. Today, the individuals who comprise the field are less homogeneous than in the past. Where once most grant professionals came from the arena of social justice, today more and more individuals bring experience as technical writers. Both groups are assets to the field but look at the field through very different lenses. Both groups operate within an ethical framework but bring unique world views of what this means.

From Practitioner to Grant Professional

Generally speaking, these individuals began their grant careers as direct-service providers in such nonprofit fields as education, health, and social justice. As a group, they were asked by their superiors to write a grant, and quickly learned of the power of grants to advance their programming. They may see grant development as a skill set or a means to an end. Their professional world view is more broad-based, with an emphasis on the program and its impact on the recipients.

From Writer to Grant Professional

Generally speaking, these grant professionals enter through the door of technical writing and journalism. They view the task from the point of view of written discourse. For the technical writer, it may not necessarily be about the beneficiaries but rather how to create a coherent response to what is being asked by the funder. They see grant development as the end game. Their professional world view is more targeted and specific.

From Recent Graduate to Grant Professional

In increasing numbers, particularly via social media, we are seeing two additional categories of individuals seeking employment in the grant field:

◆ Recent graduates of grant-related academic programs such as nonprofit management or community service

◆ Career-changers whose interest has been piqued as grantsmanship becomes a publically recognized field

Their lack of formal education in the art and science of crafting a grant application, along with a lack of a clear induction path into the field, brings a third worldview that interacts and influences the field.

All groups bring essential skills and experiences that move the grant field forward as a respected profession. Conversely, all bring gaps in knowledge that can lead to different ethical breaches involving plagiarism and confidentiality issues, or mission drift and programmatic inexperience for the technical writers and newcomers.

We know a community flourishes when it has multiple points of view and diversity within its ranks, and in this regard our profession is fortunate. However, this new face of grantsmanship also creates a dilemma. For a professional community to grow and be strong, it must operate within a common philosophical framework. We must all work together under the same banner. Without formal education and an induction path into the field, the framework must be publically shared and strongly promoted so that all understand and internalize it. Moreover, the framework must resonate with all its members and reflect their professional experiences. We must use our collective experience to advance our professional community. This task most often falls to a professional association, or, in this case, GPA. For these reasons, among others, GPA continually reviews and updates the GPA Code of Ethics to reflect this changing face.

Grant Development

Grant development is

◆ the act of writing a compelling story, and

◆ the act that creates programs.

When an Ethical Breach Befalls a GPC

Grant professionals who successfully sit for certification come to the exam with a commitment to GPCI's vision, mission, and values.

GPCI addresses ethical violations in its Grievance and Disciplinary Actions Policy. The policy exists for two primary purposes:

- To maintain and enhance the credibility of the GPC

- To provide a mechanism for consumers and others to file complaints regarding potential misconduct by a GPC

GPCI and GPA have a list of actions they may take if a member is found to have violated the code of ethics. Members and certified grant professionals should periodically review the code to ensure they do not inadvertently commit violations. However, sometimes violations do occur and the ethics committees are compelled to take action. According to GPCI, grounds for disciplinary action include but are not limited to:

- An irregular event in connection with a GPC exam, including (but not limited to) copying examination materials, causing a disruption in the testing area, and failure to abide by reasonable test administration rules

- Disclosing, publishing, reproducing, summarizing, paraphrasing, or transmitting any portion of the exam in any form or by any means, verbal, written, electronic, or mechanical, without the prior express written permission of GPCI

- Plagiarism on a grant-related article, white paper, or application, whether in whole or in part

- Providing fraudulent or misleading information on the GPC Eligibility Packet, Certification Maintenance Program (CMP) application, any grant application, or any grant report

- Gross or repeated negligence in professional work

- Proof of embezzling, theft, or other criminal act

- The conviction, plea of guilty to, or plea of *nolo contendere* to a felony or misdemeanor related to the grant profession

- Other unprofessional conduct as determined by GPCI

GPCI may impose one or more of the following sanctions for a violation of the Grievance and Disciplinary Actions Policy (abridged):

- *Censure*—Censure may be invoked with respect to professional misconduct not deemed sufficiently severe to warrant greater sanction. In the event of such a censure, the GPC would retain certification status and all associated rights and privileges, provided the grant professional complies with any requirements imposed by the GPCI board in conjunction with the censure.

- *Probation*—A respondent may be placed on probation for a period not to exceed three years. If any further professional misconduct complaints are substantiated during the period of probation, the respondent's GPC status shall be suspended or revoked, as determined by the GPCI Review Committee and the GPCI board. A GPC placed on probation would retain certification status and all rights and privileges during the period of probation, provided that the grant professional complies with any requirements imposed by the GPCI board in conjunction with the probation.

◆ *Suspension*—GPC status may be suspended for a specified period not to exceed three years based upon the severity of the professional misconduct. A GPC whose certification status is suspended shall, immediately upon such suspension, not be entitled to any of the rights and privileges of certification status during such period of suspension. On completion of the suspension period, the grant professional may apply to the GPCI board for reinstatement of GPC status.

◆ *Revocation*—GPC status may be revoked. A GPC whose certification status has been revoked shall, immediately upon revocation, no longer be entitled to any of the rights and privileges of certification status. Moreover, the (former) GPC shall not be entitled to reinstatement. Revoked certificates and letters of official award of certification must be returned to GPCI once notice is received. Notice of revocation of the credential shall be published on the GPCI website.

More information regarding GPCI's grievance process can be found at *grantcredential.org*.

The Best Defense is a Good Offense

Most ethical dilemmas don't start out as ethical dilemmas. They start out as small missteps or by not taking the time to find out if what you are doing is okay or not. Little things add up and grow. You don't want an issue to snowball into a larger problem. When the little voice creeps up inside you, listen to it and take the time to check your actions.

When grant professionals are faced with an ethical quandary, it's not usually because of anything sinister, but because they didn't realize it was a problem. While ignorance is no excuse, we encourage you to take the time to check with your colleagues often. Have lunch with another grant professional, attend a GPA chapter meeting, or attend a workshop on ethics or sound grant practices. If you see yourself in some doubtful scenarios, it's time to rethink your behavior. Of course, reading over and reflecting on the GPA Code of Ethics is a good idea, also. Read one clause per week and think about how it applies to your work.

It appears that the concept of *the best defense is a good offense* could apply here if one is to avoid a slippery slope. To this end, every grant professional's playbook should include the following elements and strategies:

◆ An understanding of your professional limits—know what you do and don't know

◆ Possession of *all* of the grant professional competencies disseminated by GPCI before offering your services (volunteer or paid) to a grant-seeking entity

◆ Knowledge of the state laws governing your grant work and recognition that state laws are rapidly changing due to the professionalization of the field

What Is Good Ethical Practice?

Good ethical practice involves periodically reviewing the GPA Code of Ethics and taking steps to mitigate any risks associated with potential ethical misconduct. You can also attend workshops or presentations on ethics and discuss these matters with your colleagues.

important

- A resume that's clear in how grant funds were raised (new funding, continued funding, formula funding, etc.). It's very easy to inadvertently misrepresent successes and experience.

- A personal resolution that the facts, figures, and information contained in a grant, of which you are the author or contributor, are conveyed accurately in both content and context

- A keen understanding of how easy it is to disclose confidential information. We are a small community that regularly interacts with our grant-seeking and grantmaking counterparts.

> **Should You Speak Up? Yes!**
>
> If you notice an organization engaging in an act that is unethical or illegal (real or perceived, intentional or inadvertent), you should share your observations with the organization.
>
> **principle**

- A clear picture of what constitutes a conflict of interest and the "game plays" to avoid them

- Knowledge that conflicts of interest are both real and perceived. Both can do real damage.

- Acknowledgement that ethics and trust work in tandem

- An honest assessment of your own values and world view. Do you engage in beliefs and behaviors that suppress cultural diversity and pluralistic values?

- The ability to articulate to a fund-seeking entity why working on a percentage basis or receiving payment from grant proceeds is not in anyone's best interest

- Recognition of how ethical dilemmas begin, and possession of the tools to mitigate them as soon as they're identified

- Understanding that ethical dilemmas don't always happen as a result of the grant professional's decisions or behaviors. Many times the challenge is precipitated by others and then becomes the problem of the grant professional.

- Full knowledge of the GPA Code of Ethics with the understanding that it is broad-based, subject to individual interpretation, and may not address all possible situations faced by the professional. If something doesn't feel right, it probably isn't.

> **More Potential Conflicts of Interest**
>
> Here are a couple more potential conflicts of interest you should consider:
>
> - Developing a grant for a family member who will directly benefit from the funding
>
> - Developing a grant that purchases goods and services from other businesses that financially benefit the grant professional
>
> **Example**

- The patience to take a deep breath and wait before addressing an ethical challenge

- In the event you inadvertently engage in unethical behavior (real or perceived), possess the strength and skills to acknowledge it, mitigate it, and commit to never doing it again.

Are You Exam Ready?

You are exam ready if you:

- ◆ Are familiar with and embrace the GPCI Vision, Mission and Values statements (located on the GPCI website at *grantcredential.org*)

- ◆ Are familiar with the GPA Code of Ethics

- ◆ Have a good understanding of the importance of ethics to society and the profession

- ◆ Have engaged in critical thinking around this topic, and understand the interplay of professional actions and professional outcomes

- ◆ Can identify characteristics of business relationships that result in conflicts of interest or give the appearance of conflicts of interest

- ◆ Can identify circumstances that mislead stakeholders, have an appearance of impropriety, profit stakeholders other than the intended beneficiaries, and appear self-serving

- ◆ Can identify the effects of choices that foster or suppress cultural diversity and pluralistic values

- ◆ Can distinguish between truthful and untruthful, and accurate and inaccurate representations in grant development, including research and writing

- ◆ Can identify issues, effects, and countermeasures relevant to grant professionals' individual heritages, backgrounds, knowledge, and experiences, as they may affect the grant development process

- ◆ Can identify funding sources that may present conflicts of interest for specific grant-seekers and applicants

- ◆ Can identify issues and practices pertinent to communicating information that may be considered privileged, proprietary, and confidential

- ◆ Can identify unethical and illegal expenditures in a budget

- ◆ Can distinguish between ethical and unethical methods of payment for the grant-development process

- ◆ Can distinguish between ethical and unethical commitment, performance, and reporting of activities funded by a grant

Chapter Seven

Professional Practices

IN THIS CHAPTER

- ···➤ The meaning of professionalism and professionalization
- ···➤ Roadblocks preventing the field from achieving professional status
- ···➤ The importance of certification to advancing the field
- ···➤ How being engaged in the profession advances the grant field

Competency seven requires us to possess the knowledge, attitudes, and behaviors that raise our level of professionalism. It takes a critical look at how our professional philosophies and beliefs shape the public's understanding of the grant profession. This chapter not only contributes to your readiness to take the GPC exam, it also suggests talking points for the all-important "what I do for a living" elevator speech. As in **Chapter Six**, this chapter has very few facts for you to memorize. Rather, its content must be internalized so it can benefit you *and* the field.

Professionalism is more than a critical definition, more than a skill, and more than a credential. We know that good habits are the foundation of professionalism, and that knowing our craft and its rules and regulations are important skills. Every grant professional spends time determining professional goals. But professionalism is more than about us as individuals. It's about our role within the profession and how our understanding of professionalism directly impacts the field.

In order to engage in professional growth, we must understand the meaning of professionalism in its fullest context. To do this, we must start with a discussion that looks at the concept of "profession," our role within it, and the pesky roadblocks that seem to get in our way.

Let's begin with some simple definitions.

According to Mr. Webster, Mr. Oxford, and Ms. Merriam, a *profession* is a paid occupation, especially one that involves prolonged training and a formal qualification.

The degree of expertise and complexity involved in the work task distinguishes a profession from an occupation.

Professionalism is More Than Being Professional

GPA and GPCI describe the work we do as rich and complex. We, as professionals, view the work as rich and complex. Our field, on the other hand is "littered" with public statements that minimize the work as something to be learned "overnight." We see it over and over again on LinkedIn via the age-old question of "How do I become a grant writer?" We will discuss this in greater detail later in this chapter.

A *professional* is a person who is engaged in a specified activity, and viewed as one's main paid occupation rather than as a pastime. According to the National Center for Educational Statistics (1997), "Recognized professionals require completion of an officially sanctioned or accredited training program and passage of examinations to obtain credentials in order to practice." To be a professional, according to GPA and GPCI, you must have

- ◆ a level or degree of competency and skill, as identified by the field *and* demonstrated through professional certification;

- ◆ an internalization that, as professionals, we have an obligation to continue to enhance those competencies and skills; and

- ◆ a recognition that learning is acquired from our peers *and* our stakeholders.

Merriam-Webster describes the term *professionalize* as the act of making an activity into a job that requires special education, training, or skill. In tandem, *professionalization* is a process whereby occupations seek to upgrade their status by adopting organizational and occupational attributes and traits attributed to professions.

You may ask how the sociological concept of professionalization found its way into this chapter. Quite simply, it provides a framework for GPA and GPCI's overall approach to professionalism.

Caution: Roadblocks Ahead

Why do we struggle to define who we are and what we do? We struggle due to behaviors and beliefs imposed on us by ourselves, others who dabble in the "idea of grants" and remain firmly affixed to the fringes of the profession, and a public that lacks awareness of what we do.

Let's review some of the more pronounced professional roadblocks created by us and others that prevent the field from achieving full professionalization.

Roadblock Number One: Inability to Establish with Authority *"Who We Are" and "What We Do"*

The vast majority of grant professionals hold academic degrees, many of them at the highest levels. We often enter the field with distinguished service records in the nonprofit sector, including education, medicine, science, and communications. Yet, we trip over ourselves, contradict, and even correct each other regarding our particular professional "term of choice." To illustrate, let's review this simple two-pronged top-of-mind awareness (TOMA) question.

Here's a quiz that gets to how you refer to yourself and how the public refers to you. Choose any or all of the following responses.

❑ Grant writer

❑ Grant developer

❑ Grant professional

❑ Grant strategist

❑ Grant specialist

❑ ... and as part of doing that I also write grants

❑ All of the above

❑ None of the above

❑ Some but not all

❑ All but not some

❑ Really, do we have to have this discussion?

> ### Top-of-Mind Awareness
>
> Top-of-mind awareness (TOMA) is the first thought, visual, or brand that comes to mind when someone is asked an unprompted question about a category; usually associated with marketing.
>
>

In answer to how you refer to yourself, you may have chosen all eleven options, perhaps only two or three, or even the lone "grant professional." However, in terms of how you believe the public refers to you, we suspect you probably chose just one answer: grant writer.

If we can't agree on what to call ourselves, it only stands to reason that the public will be lost, too. This fundamental roadblock should be a signal to our professional associations as they navigate the professionalization continuum. They need to identify, validate, and promote a standardized term to be used by the field. (Did you know that, in this manual, we chose "grant professional" and "grant profession" over "grants professional" and "grants profession"? Yep! We had to think through the terminology in writing this manual. What do you think of our choice?)

GPA and GPCI have made great progress to legitimize the grant field, but there's still work to do! We must all work together to fully develop core terminology.

Roadblock Number Two: Lack of an Agreed-upon Elevator Speech

How often is it that someone asks you, "So, what do you do?" and you immediately have a private conversation with yourself? "Should I say *grant writer* or *grant professional*? They'll understand *writer* better than *professional*. Everyone uses *writer*. But if I say *writer*, it really doesn't reflect what I do. But (internal heavy sigh) which is more important to this conversation?"

Regardless of your ultimate reply, which follow-up response do you most often experience from this inquiring mind?

◆ "Huh?" followed by a blank stare.

◆ "Oh, a grant writer. I always thought that would be a nice skill to acquire. Is it something you can show me how to do?"

◆ "So you work on commission. What do you get—a percentage of the grant? You must be rich."

◆ "Show me the money (ha, ha, ha)!"

Since we're a part of multi-billion-dollar field that affects millions of individuals daily, we should be able to easily explain the important work we do. It should roll off our tongues like sweet nectar, be clearly illustrated as if by the strokes of a well-worn pallet knife … or at least be a simply-stated description that goes beyond "I write text." This articulation should be especially simple. After all, the field, through psychometric protocols, has defined, vetted, and published a full range of competencies and skills required for successful pursuit of grant funding.

Roadblock Number Three: Lack of Grant-specific Academic Credentials and an Unrefined Induction System

> ### Who Created the GPCI Competencies? *You did!*
>
> Neither GPA nor GPCI created or developed the GPC Competencies. They are the by-product of a comprehensive psychometric undertaking that included three field surveys, one job analysis, several focus groups, and specific input from seventy-five subject-matter experts. In other words, you and your professional peers developed the GPCI Competencies.
>
> **principle**

Consider the following "getting started" question posted on LinkedIn, which surfaces with great frequency: "Hi. I'm new to the group and have been thinking about trying my hand at writing proposals for a while now. Is there any formal training that anyone would recommend over just diving in and doing it?"

How would you respond?

- ◆ Workshop or course from the Foundation Center
- ◆ Workshop or course from the Grantsmanship Center
- ◆ Learn on the job by volunteering with an emerging nonprofit
- ◆ Attend the annual GPA Conference
- ◆ All of the above
- ◆ None of the above

The "All of the above" answer is the answer of choice 99 percent of the time, as these are the options that first come to mind, and are pretty much what is available to us. Yet, many of us aspire to answer "None of the above" because... because what we seek is an academic credential, which is missing from this list. Also absent from this list is a training mechanism that takes longer than a week to acquire. Instead, responses reflect "try this," "good luck with your grant career pursuits," or this actual response: "The best way is to write a grant. Then you basically know if you're cut out to do it as a profession." The question then becomes, *at whose expense?*

Without a recognized professional standard or license or academic credential, anyone can simply hang out the proverbial shingle. Unfortunately, many of these self-declared "experts" and their reflections find their way into the literature, blogs, and those infamous infomercials.

You'd be surprised at what you'd find when you google *grants, grant writing,* and *grantsmanship*. The following reflection is from Vanessa S. O'Neal, the founder of the National Society of Grant Writing Professionals at *wango.org*:

> *Grant writing, although a very technical form of writing and an extremely important position within any nonprofit, is not a profession; it is a position. Most grant writers are not just grant writers. They are board members, executive directors, fundraising specialists, and so forth.*

What happens when people believe that grant development is a simple skill set rather than a complex, multidimensional body of knowledge and skills acquired through training and experience? Without a belief that our work is a bona fide profession, we may not feel the need to invest in an association, promote ethical and professional standards, or seek opportunities for professional development.

Without growth and exposure to current trends, we will continue to send a message to the public that perpetuates a very narrow view of the field. When this occurs, the field is hampered in its movement toward full professionalization and we're back to square one.

Fortunately, there's a clear path to alter public perception and establish the field as an understood and respected profession: professionalization. This sociological approach provides us with a roadmap to guide us along a constructive path.

Professionalization of the Grant Field—Clearing the Roadblocks

If our field is to advance as a profession, GPA and we, as its members, must have a keen understanding of professionalization's framework. Professionalization provides us with clear benchmarks toward greater professionalism. It helps us create statements to talk about our work in a collective voice (our elevator speech), which leads to increased public awareness of the importance *and* complexity of the grant field. It helps us recognize and mitigate public *and* self-created roadblocks, and it ties our own professional goals to the goals of the profession.

Credit for the concept of professionalization is often given to H. Wilensky, who introduced it to the academic world in the mid-1960s. However, the concept was first discussed scientifically as early as the 1920s and alluded to as early as the 19th century.

The concept of professionalization is not complicated. Its key elements state that professionalization:

> ◆ Is not acquired but, as proposed by Nicholas C. Burbules and Kathleen Densmore in a 1991 article, "The Limits of Making Teaching a Profession," a dynamic social process in a continual state of flux in that it never stops moving

> ◆ Operates on a continuum with well-recognized and undisputed professions on one end and the least-skilled unattractive occupations on the other

> ◆ Adheres to specific criteria that move an occupation from one end of the spectrum to the other

> ### Factors Holding Back the Grant Profession
>
> Despite our progress, there are four fundamental roadblocks that still hinder our achievement of full professionalization. They are:
>
> ◆ An inability to adopt and internalize a noun in which to call ourselves—among ourselves and with our stakeholders
>
> ◆ Consensus and internalization among our stakeholders (including ourselves) as to our purpose in society
>
> ◆ Consensus and internalization among our stakeholders (including ourselves) as to the scope and complexity of the work
>
> ◆ A belief that grant development is something one can learn and do to earn money during hard financial times
>
>

Twelve criteria define the process of professionalization. Let's look at where we fall on the professionalization continuum.

Professionalization Criteria—How Do We Fare?

To determine where the grant field falls on the professionalization continuum, we must look at it from three points of view:

◆ What is factual

◆ What our field's most outspoken contributors believe to be factual

◆ The unknowing public's perception

Let's look at twelve criteria for professionalization and see where we are:

Grant Professionalization Criteria	
Criteria	Criteria Met?
Creation of a full-time occupation. Are there job descriptions for full-time work?	Yes
Systematic theory. Are there abstract concepts, recognized competencies?	Yes
Establishment of a training school. Can you receive an academic degree in grant development?	Not Yet
Formation of an association. Did it include a name change?	Yes
Code of Ethics. Does it have a public statement of duty?	Yes
Credentials. Does it have professional recognition through certification?	Yes
Induction. Does it have a mechanism to transition new professionals into the field?	No
Compensation. Does it have a range of salary and benefits that allow for gainful employment?	Yes
Continuing professional development. Is there ongoing availability?	Yes
Authority. Does it have influence in national and state-driven policy making?	Not Yet
Community sanction. Is there public recognition of the standards promulgated by the field?	No
Culture. Is there evidence of a collective identity, such as established networks?	Yes

With eight criteria met, two under construction, and two not yet achieved, our place along the professionalization continuum is strong.

So, in terms of professionalization, the four outstanding criteria needing attention include:

◆ Accredited training program—establishment of an academic degree for becoming a grant professional

◆ Induction—establishment of a process whereby one enters the grant field

◆ Authority—establishment of a particular entity as the go-to authority on all things grants

◆ Community sanction—education of the stakeholders and the general public regarding the importance and complexity of the field

A true grant professional should be familiar with these criteria and create a professional portfolio that demonstrates accomplishment or engagement in as many of them as possible.

The Critical Role Certification Plays in Professionalism and Achieving Full Professionalization

No discussion regarding professionalism is complete without talking about the importance of certification and defining what is an authentic professional credential.

Why Certify?

The following excerpt, reprinted from the GPCI website at *grantcredential.org,* addresses the importance of certification:

GPCI is dedicated to the public good and so believes that it is imperative that as the field emerges, it does so with the consumer situated front and center. It believes that it is essential for the nonprofit community, as well as the community-at-large, to understand the role grant professionals play in the overall health of a nonprofit organization, and the power it has over the outcomes of its fund-seeking.

Certification is one way to promulgate these core values. According to the GPCI website:

Independently established credibility stands as one of the main benefits of a nationally-recognized certification/credential. For fields such as ours where there is no recognized academic degree, certification is the only authoritative, independent measure available by which to determine a person's experience, skill, and knowledge base as defined by our peers.

Not All Certificates are Created Equal—Know the Difference

We know that our readers appreciate the importance of certification and understand its many nuances. But it can be challenging to explain these concepts. The following comments on social media sites are great examples:

- ◆ "I've been writing grants for years now and no one has asked me if I'm certified. So, it's not necessary. Besides, the certificate providers are just making up questions to make money."

- ◆ "I would like to get certified—which certificate is the best?"

- ◆ "Hi. I already got my certificate, now how do I get started in the field?"

None of these popular questions reflects an understanding of certification. How would you reply to these individuals?

As grant professionals, we must know the difference between a certificate of completion, academic classwork leading to a certificate, and professional certification—and be able to articulate the differences to others.

Engaging in Professional Behavior

To be a professional means to "engage in professional activities." According to GPA and GPCI, professional activity is achieved by engagement in three primary activity streams, specifically those that:

- ◆ Promote the professionalization milestones our field has already accomplished

- ◆ Allow us to work with our professional associations to achieve the outstanding professionalization criteria

- ◆ Enhance our abilities to be more outstanding grant professionals, traditionally referred to as continuing education

Grant professionals who are certified by GPCI are expected to participate in ongoing professional development throughout their tenure as grant professionals. To promote life-long learning and enhanced professional demeanor and skill, GPCI established the Certification Maintenance Program (CMP). The goal of the CMP is to assure the continuing competence of every Grant Professional Certified (GPC), including adherence to professional standards and the code of ethics.

At its most basic level, GPCI seeks to ensure that GPCs continue to:

◆ Obtain current professional development information

◆ Explore new knowledge in specific content areas

◆ Master new skills and techniques related to the grant profession

◆ Expand approaches to effective grant development and management

◆ Further develop professional judgment

◆ Conduct professional practice in an ethical and appropriate manner

GPA and GPCI, though, recognized early on that professionalism should reflect more than "keeping current" and enhancing personal professional skills. It means being involved in the profession and serving as "ambassadors" for the field to our stakeholders and the general public.

In support of this philosophy, the GPC Certification Maintenance Program encourages, through its point system, activities that "give back" and help shape the future of the field. CMP requires you, as a GPC, to engage in no fewer than two of the following categories as part of your professional development:

◆ Continuing education (workshops, seminars, conferences, webinars, etc.)

◆ Advanced degrees and/or related professional credentials (CFRE, content-specific, etc.)

◆ Obtaining or serving as a mentor

◆ Contributing to the field through the publication of articles, books, teaching or presenting at conferences, serving as an editor, etc.

◆ Professional service by serving on GPA or related boards or committees, or by being a member of GPA and an affiliate chapter

◆ Giving back through community service

> **Recertification—A Certification Requirement!**
>
> Within a three-year period, GPC recertification candidates must engage in no fewer than 105 hours of profession-related activities. In many but not all cases, one hour of activity is assigned one "CMP point." The CMP Manual is available on the GPCI website at *grantcredential.org*.
>
>

A grant professional believes, acknowledges, and articulates to others that what we do is more than a simple skill set. It is a bona fide profession that has significant impact on the world and its citizens.

In this chapter, we looked at why being a professional is more than paying for a membership and mining continuing education credits. It's about sharing the same "elevator speech" when describing our work, understanding the importance of promoting certification, and giving back to the field and the beneficiaries we serve. Professionalism is more than knowledge—it's a habit!

What's exciting is the myriad of accomplishments the field has achieved in a relatively short period of time. Establishment of certification was a major "jump-start." The fact that professionals such as you are taking a major step to ramp up your level of public professionalism is the most exciting thought of all. Best wishes on your upcoming exam!

Are You Exam Ready?

You are exam ready if you:

◆ Have engaged in some level of critical thinking around the topic of "how do I view my work as a grant professional"

◆ Understand the importance of being involved in the professional association as a means of growing the profession

◆ Understand how growing the profession benefits the individual and the constituents we serve

◆ Can answer these essential questions:

❖ What are some essential qualities of a professional?

❖ What should the field, GPA, and you, the individual, do to strengthen the field's stature as a profession?

❖ Why is this important?

❖ What is the definition of professionalization?

❖ What criteria determine whether the work a group of people perform is an occupation or a profession?

❖ Where along the professionalization continuum does the grant field lie?

❖ What criteria are still outstanding in the grant field?

❖ What role do social media and distance learning play in continuing education and advancing the field?

❖ Why is GPA important to you and the field?

❖ What are three major contributions GPA has made to the field?

❖ Why are you a member (or not a member) of GPA?

❖ What do you believe should be GPA's number one focus as a grant association?

❖ What volunteer opportunities are available at GPA or GPCI? Is there a good fit for you?

Recommended Professional Behaviors

If you are interested in being professional and engaged, and looking to stay invested in our rich profession, we recommend the following:

◆ Participate in professional organizations and networks

◆ Keep the professional association accountable to the basic tenets of professionalization

◆ Engage, post, correct, and guide others on social media channels

◆ Don't let nonprofessionals speak on your behalf and define the field

◆ Stay current

principle

   ❖   What is the definition of continuing education?

   ❖   What continuing education topics would be of benefit to a grant professional and the field? What topics are you qualified to teach or facilitate?

◆ Are able to identify three ways in which you can engage in professional development that results in personal growth and advances the field

◆ Can identify advantages of participating in continuing education and various grant review processes

◆ Can identify advantages of participating in professional organizations that offer growth opportunities and advance the profession

◆ Can identify how grant professionals' networks (such as listserves and community alliances) enhance individuals' professional growth and advance the profession

◆ Can identify strategies that grant professionals use in building social capital to benefit their communities and society at large

Chapter Eight

Relationships! Relationships! Relationships!

IN THIS CHAPTER

- ---➔ What are mutually beneficial relationships?

- ---➔ Who should be building relationships with funders?

- ---➔ Effective relationships are effective for a reason

- ---➔ Are you a relationship-a-holic?

This chapter covers a review of the following competency: knowledge of methods and strategies that cultivate and maintain relationships between fund-seeking and recipient organizations and funders. We could have called this chapter, "Love Thy Grantor: Building Effective Relationships with Grantmakers."

One letter of the alphabet can make a lot of difference. There's a reason why it's called GPC (Grant Professional Certified) and not GWC (Grant Writer Certified). The "P" for "professional" in the GPC acronym covers a lot more than just the actual writing of a grant proposal.

The best-written proposal in the world can fall flat in today's super-competitive funding arena without a connection to the program officer, board of trustees, or family foundation. In a world of online applications and webinar technical training, it's easy to forget that there's a person or a review committee of several people behind these virtual gates. Building working relationships and making meaningful connections over time is what helps a grant program grow. This ultimately creates more positive change in the communities you serve as a grant professional.

Even though the inevitable rejection letter or email may bring you down, it's important to remember that we're all in this together. Private and corporate foundations, and federal, state, and local granting agencies, are required by law to grant a certain amount of funding each year. Of course, they are not required to give that funding to your organization or client! But they couldn't exist without grant professionals like you who help connect them to nonprofits and educational institutions doing great work in their communities.

What Are Mutually Beneficial Relationships?

The first step to mutually beneficial relationships is to realize that relationships, like partnerships, should not be one-sided. All parties to the relationship should bring something to the table. Each partner should also benefit in some way, even if the benefit isn't entirely tangible. In this chapter, we'll identify the characteristics of mutually beneficial relationships between fund seekers and funders.

Fostering an open, appropriate, and regular communication style with a funder helps to clarify each other's focus areas and accomplishments. This communication goes beyond meeting deadlines for submitting high-quality proposals and required reports on or before deadlines—although these are essential first steps!

In fact, timeliness is the key to a mutually beneficial relationship between grant-seekers and grantmakers. For example, don't wait until a day before the grant deadline to contact a foundation about your proposal. Or, even worse, don't call the foundation two days after the deadline to discuss the finer points of your recently submitted proposal, or to demand to know its status. Part of your research process for new and existing funders should be to understand, note, and time your communications around the funder's grant cycle.

Professionalism and respect are also cornerstones to building mutually beneficial relationships with funders. As grant professionals, we're often under tremendous pressure to meet challenging revenue goals. This kind of pressure has driven some to push too hard for connection or communication on their own timetable—a strategy that has ultimately backfired.

Making the Ask: Right Person, Right Time!

During a workshop on grantsmanship, a funder told the story of a new executive director who attended the funeral of the mother of the head of a local family foundation. In his zeal to get funding for his organization, he offered his condolences to the mourning son and family and then passed on a proposal to them as they prepared to leave the cemetery. And no, that wasn't a successful approach for the ambitious but misguided nonprofit leader, who cost his organization any chance of future funding from the family foundation.

 stories from the real world

---

For a grant professional truly dedicated to fostering strong funding relationships, even a rejection from a foundation can be a tool to further communication and perhaps future funding. Remember, this may be a "no for now," especially if this was the first application to this particular funder. Assuming the grant proposal met all the requirements, matched the focus area, and was clear and compelling, it could be easy to take rejection personally. Try your best to deal with this in a healthy, productive way. If that doesn't work, then go ahead and throw a hissy fit in the privacy of your office. Or "walk it off" if that's more your style.

Whatever you do, don't take out your hard feelings on the funder. An angry voice mail or email is guaranteed only to ensure future funding failure!

Another key characteristic to establishing mutually beneficial relationships between a funder and grantee is matching the level of communication and the message to the most appropriate person from the grantee and/or grant-seeking organization. For smaller nonprofits with one or two people on staff, the choice is straightforward. For larger nonprofits, or for consultants, discerning the right "messenger" may not be so easy. In these cases, it really depends of the type of funding organization involved.

For example, initial cultivation or introductory meetings with a foundation large enough to have staff could involve the executive director, a board member, and possibly a development director. This is particularly important for foundations that don't accept unsolicited proposals, but it's a good rule of thumb for most others as well. Following an invitation to submit a proposal, the grant professional usually handles the day-to-day communications with the program officer throughout the proposal process. A grantee's senior leaders (executive directors, board chairs) are the best choices to officially recognize grant awards through check presentations and other activities.

The grant professional would most likely handle reporting and site visits directly related to the current grant cycle. Near the end of the grant cycle is a great time to involve senior leaders in a more informal site visit, lunch, or meeting to discuss future partnerships.

Who Should Be Building Relationships with Funders?

The question comes up frequently, "Who should be contacting the funders?" The answer varies by organization and circumstances. It's important for you and your organization to determine the rules of cultivation, recognition, and stewardship that suit your mission, culture, and values.

Hundreds of helpful articles and books exist on how to best research prospects and steward them once they've donated. Technique and theories abound, some useful, others not so much. But really, the best way boils down to three simple words—ask and listen. We recommend you read as much as you can, because if you've met one funder, you've met one funder.

Some methods and strategies are spelled out during the grant cycle itself, especially for government agencies and well-established corporate foundations. Award letters from these funders often come with grant agreements specifying how and when to refer to the funder and when to consult them in advance. Other funders may request anonymity as a condition of current and future giving. If you're not a one-person shop, be sure to communicate this clearly to your development and marketing departments. Make notes in your donor database about these specific requests and include a tickler file for donor lists in your annual report or other official communications. Again, when in doubt—ask and listen.

> ### Complaining Isn't Constructive Feedback
>
> In a GPA regional grants conference, a program officer in a community foundation panel related that as one of the few funders in a mostly rural area, he may receive hundreds of applications in single cycle without hope of funding even half of them. He shared that after contacting those who did not receive funding, he inevitably receives several angry emails.
>
> While most of the audience chuckled in disbelief, at least one other panelist nodded in agreement that she, too, had received that type of communication from unsuccessful applicants. Not a single panelist said that negative communication swayed any of them into making the grant to a grouchy applicant after all.
>
> practical tip

Recognition Is Always a Good Thing, Right?

While it's true that most corporate donors are comfortable with public recognition and many family foundations may choose to remain anonymous, it's dangerous to assume that they all fall into one of these two broad categories. It's poor and lazy stewardship as well. A quick call or email is often all it takes to clarify what works best for a donor. Be sure to keep checking in outside of the often frenzied grant cycles. Donor preferences can change over time, particularly with corporate funders.

For years, a tech company headquartered near the nonprofit where one of us worked was a steady, dependable funder. Following the basic proposal letter that was sent in September, the organization would receive a generous check by mid-December. The foundation manager refused any official recognition other than a photo at the check presentation and a mention in the donor list in the annual report. The same amount and the same modest recognition continued for three years until a larger firm from Silicon Valley purchased the tech company.

The foundation manager retired and the newly merged company began a much more involved connection with the nonprofit. The grants grew alongside new volunteer teams and employee giving drives. When asked if they would like a plaque or trophy along with regular volunteer certificates, the answer was a resounding "Yes!" The team stepped up its recognition with thank you cards handmade by child volunteers and was invited in turn to annual employee parties and other events. Asking and listening resulted in a more engaged funder and increased support for our cause.

It's easy to slide into a sort of "call and response" with grantmakers. And some funders still prefer it that way. They call, or issue RFPs (request for proposals) and deadlines, and you respond with a proposal or report. And it ends there. These days, that practice can be a costly mistake, and one that separates a grant writer from a grant professional.

Grantmakers truly want to make a difference, or at the very least are legally obligated to distribute funds to do so. Maintaining authentic, appropriate, and timely communication and recognition helps you do both. To build these mutually beneficial relationships, you don't have to be the extremely extroverted "life

---

Fostering Deep Connections

Some aspects of relationship building aren't intuitive. Sometimes we need help discovering ways we can grow relationships. Here are some ideas to foster deeper connections with your funders.

◆ Invite foundation directors, program officers and/or board members to speak at your GPA chapter meetings and regional and national GPA conferences.

◆ Host issue-oriented forums for funders every year on timely topics and trends that directly affect the work of your nonprofit and those you serve.

◆ Coordinate more informal one-on-one coffees or lunches with foundation leaders and your executive director or board chair, outside of the grant cycle.

◆ Forward to your contacts photos, posts, or related articles about the funder or about its funding priorities.

◆ Interview funders for GPA newsletters or for articles in the *GPA Journal* about best practices or funding trends.

◆ Extend team volunteer service opportunities, especially to corporate donors with offices or headquarters in your service area.

◆ Make a short video with program staff and volunteers thanking the foundation for its grant and send it to the program officer. After securing its permission, post it to your social media network.

practical tip

of the party." You just need to think outside the grant cycle and remember that behind the applications, official announcements, and imposing offices are people.

Effective Relationships Are Effective for a Reason

Effective relationships are often effective because the grant-seeking organization has created effective collaborations with other organizations which are more appropriate to the funder's missions and goals. The new partnership's programs and services are very attractive to funders.

The most seasoned grant professional is someone who's least likely to chase money. That may not make sense at first. Isn't a grant professional's primary role to secure grant funding? Yes! Winning well-planned, appropriate grants that help better serve the target communities should be "job one." But throwing together proposal after proposal that tries to shoehorn programs and services ill-matched to a funder's focus just because six-figure or more awards are available is neither efficient nor effective. And it's not in the best interest of the organization or that of our clients if you're chasing one restricted grant after another that aren't clear fits with your mission or strategic plan.

> ### Which Is First: Collaboration or the Need for Collaboration?
>
> Don't let deadlines determine your collaborations. One of us received a call once from a local nonprofit that wanted a letter of support for a proposal they had to get in the very next day. We've all had our backs against a wall against a looming deadline at some point in our careers, so the caller's request was listened to intently. His program may have been a good fit with one of our service areas, but our organizations had never collaborated before. Less than twenty-four hours before a major deadline was not the time to start working together or even drafting a memorandum of understanding or letter of support that suggested we intended to work together.
>
>  practical tip

We're not fans of chasing money. Winning well-planned, appropriate grants that help better serve our community? Count us in!

Let the mission and services of your nonprofit and those of organizations in your geographic area or in your field locally, regionally, or nationally lead the development of true, effective collaborations. They take time and effort for you and for your program staff and leaders.

Before you talk to potential collaborators, think about these key questions:

◆ Which agencies are doing a good job of providing similar services?

◆ Does my organization have the time and ability to work closely with another organization? This includes sharing or expanding programs and services as well as tracking expenses and reporting outcomes.

◆ Are there organizations that receive funding from the same foundations or grantmakers for the same type of work?

◆ Would the expansion of programs, services, or client base from this potential collaboration merit the time and effort needed?

◆ Are we comfortable with sharing potential funders, program materials, and other potentially proprietary information?

What Guides Successful Collaborations?

One of the most rewarding and challenging experiences one of us had was with a collaboration that involved medical, legal, and academic institutions working together to provide services for medically fragile children from low-income families. All three organizations were effective, efficient, and committed financially and with staff and space to make this important work happen. The rewarding part is that we raised more than a million dollars as a group. The challenging part is that we raised more than a million dollars as a group.

In a series of meetings we hammered out which organization was the best lead agency for each major ask. We shared names of funders we had in common to best raise money for this project while also keeping our regular grants coming in. While we're proud of what this group accomplished together, the success of this collaboration stemmed from first fully developing the concept and then assigning location and responsibilities across departments and institutions. Finally, we matched the program to potential funders—not the other way around. We weren't chasing money; together we were matching funders' focus areas to better serve the clients we had in common.

practical tip

Are You a Relationship-a-holic?

Grant relationships should be established well in advance of the deadline. Start your relationships with an open mind, ditch the hidden agendas, and be a listener.

Grants require the kinds of relationships for quality proposal development. If you've been in the grant profession for a while, you've seen a pattern around collaborations and partnerships. Many grant applications require community input, letters of support, partners, and collaborations.

We recommend getting to know anyone in your community who is a grant seeker. Learning about your grant competition is important for many reasons. It's valuable to know about all the services available for your clients, avoiding duplicative services, keeping your fees for services in line, and effective use of critical financial resources. The best case for getting to know your competition is to find ways to collaborate. Most funders prefer to award grants to good partner organizations.

The fastest way to destroy a relationship is to eliminate trust. One of the most common ways to do this is to show up only when you need a partner, a letter of support, or grant funds, then disappear after the grant application is submitted. Don't be a relationship-a-holic.

Politics of Relationships!

Relationships are the social mechanism by which people seek to gain power, influence, or control. Most relationships are genuine and based on mutual trust. Other relationships, such as those with lobbyists, are based on money and influence.

Politics are the acts of influence and persuasion. Politicians try to influence people to vote for them on Election Day. Politicians persuade their peers to support key initiatives, proposed bills, laws, and policies and to vote legislation into effect. In many circumstances, politics is another term for an informal barter system of influence.

When you're cultivating and maintaining relationships, it's okay to play politics, but be cautious. Some people may maintain a relationship with you for reasons that may not be clear on the surface. Relationships, like friendships, should be balanced, neither side giving all the time and neither side taking every time. We recommend you evaluate your relationships from time to time and shed any that feel one-sided.

Building solid working relationships with funders and collaborators is the key to successful grant development and to fundraising in general. Taking the time to ask, listen, and think outside the grant cycle will help you grow as a grant professional and, more importantly, secure new and repeat grant dollars that will ultimately better serve your community.

Are You Exam Ready?

You are exam ready if you can identify:

◆ Characteristics of mutually beneficial relationships between fund seekers and funders

◆ Strategies to determine approaches that suit your organization's mission, culture, and values

◆ Methods to help fund-seeking organizations create effective collaborations with other organizations that align with funders' missions and goals

◆ Methods of relationship cultivation, communication, recognition, and stewardship that might appeal to specific funders

Chapter Nine

The Writing Prompt

IN THIS CHAPTER

---→ Writing a convincing case for funding

---→ Strategies to organize a clearly-stated case for funding

---→ Making a persuasive argument for funding

---→ Consumer-centric as opposed to institution-centric writing

Competency nine requires grant professionals to know and execute the elements that make up a well-crafted need statement. This chapter makes an important assumption—that you, as the reader, bring a good (certainly beyond basic) understanding of the conventions of English grammar and composition. As such, we will not focus on the mechanics of writing.

Rather, in this chapter we will review the elements that create a compelling and organized *case statement*, referred to as the written prompt in the GPC exam. Also referred to as a letter of inquiry or preapplication, a case statement is usually, but not always, between two and three pages. In this chapter, we'll use the term *case statement* to describe the written prompt component of the exam.

For such a small part of the overall grant application process, the case statement really does carry a big punch. It's the first impression your reader forms about your organization. There's an informal saying in the grant field—don't write with EGO, meaning don't cause your reader's "eyes to glaze over." Use these few important pages to set your stage for what's to come. Make it count!

About the Written Prompt

The written prompt represents the second section of the GPCI exam. The examinee has ninety minutes to write a persuasive argument that would help lead a funder to award a grant. More specifically, the written prompt should leave the reviewer understanding:

◆ Why there's a problem or need, and why the reader should care

◆   How the applicant agency will address the need (via a program or project)

◆   Why the applicant agency is best equipped to mitigate the need or problem

Six criteria form the scoring rubric for the written prompt. They include the abilities to:

◆   Make a persuasive argument (34 percent)

◆   Organize ideas appropriately (22 percent)

◆   Convey ideas clearly (18 percent)

◆   Use information provided (12 percent)

◆   Use conventional Standard English (10 percent)

◆   Follow formatting requirements (4 percent)

Please Pick Me! Organizing a Case Statement

A strong case statement includes three primary categories: the draw, the need/solution, and the closing. Within each category are suggested talking points. Grant developers often focus only on one category to the detriment of the overall case statement.

Key Elements of the Case Statement

Category One: The Draw

◆   Draw them in with a reason to want to read more, such as a compelling scene, example, or surprising fact.

◆   Share a bit about the applicant—you'd be surprised at how often people only give the applicant's name.

Category Two: The Need and Solution

◆   Convey the need using Credibility/Logic/Emotion (Ethos/Logos/Pathos) through tables and charts, needs assessments, and testimonials.

◆   Connect need with solution (cause ⇨ effect ⇨ solution).

◆   Identify and anticipate reasons for refusal—and rebut them.

Category Three: The Closing

◆   Forecast what will happen without the solution.

◆   Repeat key ideas or statements.

◆   Remind the reader why the applicant is the best choice.

important

Creating a separate paragraph for each of the previous points isn't necessary for the written prompt, as we'll see in some of the examples below.

Strengths and Weaknesses of Four Case Statements

As grant professionals, we're aware that our field consists of highly competent professionals as well as the uninformed person who believes anyone can write a proposal and win a grant award.

To illustrate this wide range of ability and understanding, we've provided excerpts from four grant applications. Applicants were asked to provide a two- to three-page narrative in conjunction with a call for proposals for a $90,000 grant targeting homelessness prevention programs. The four applications are organized by the case statement key elements (Draw, Need, and Conclusion).

A brief critique of each text's strengths and weaknesses follows the text. As you look at these examples, consider how you would rate these responses. Do you note other strengths and weaknesses not mentioned in the critiques?

> ### What's in the Case Statement?
>
> Never assume a potential funder will read a cover letter or look at any of your attachments. Every *essential* fact it needs to know should be included in the case statement. In many ways it reflects the elements we see in a press release.
>
> practical tip

The Draw

We *all* know that a grant professional must be able to convince a funder that the project/program is worth funding. But, before we can do that, we must get its attention. How we do that depends on a number of factors: the funding source, how well we know the funder, the anticipated reader (e.g., content expert, funding staff, board member, etc.), and, frankly, how much we know and care about a given topic.

Within the first two to three paragraphs, you should have mentioned in a compelling way—at minimum and not necessarily in this order—the following elements:

- ◆ The name of the applicant agency and one simple fact that puts an initial face on the entity
- ◆ A prevailing problem, a cause for the problem, and its impact on the entity's beneficiaries
- ◆ If appropriate, the entity's proposed solution in one or two sentences

Sometimes, in our zeal to spin a story or share our concern for a need, we overlook talking about the overarching problem, and instead jump right into describing the need. In tandem, we also overlook connecting the dots between "need" and "solution," which we will review in greater detail in the next section. In the meantime, give some thought to these five opening "draw" statements.

Applicant 1

The individuals that the I'm Finally Home! organization serves are homeless and living on the streets. This is an important need for our community–to help those who do not have permanent homes and who are sleeping on the street. We want to help these men and women to have the American dream.

Strengths	◆ It mentions the name of the applicant.
Weaknesses	◆ Poorly written. The reader fears this will be a long, painful application.

Applicant 2

Homelessness in the community where I'm Finally Home! is located is a big problem with an estimated 10 percent of the community not having permanent homes. These individuals not only live in poverty, but also have many other issues. Over 60 percent of the homeless population in our area are estimated to have mental illness and nearly the same amount have less than a high school diploma.

Strengths	◆ It mentions the name of the applicant.
Weaknesses	◆ It talks about a vague place.
	◆ Not a distinct geographic area.
	◆ The reader worries about EGO (eyes glazing over) because all the statistics lack a connecting visual.
	◆ Percentage of how many not tied to a number—10 percent of two or two hundred?
	◆ It provides the statistics before executing the "draw."

Applicant 3

Over the past five years, I'm Finally Home!, a social service organization serving individuals who do not have permanent, stable housing in Happyfield, has seen an increase in the need for services. Our community is a midsized city that has seen its homeless population rise to over the national average for communities of similar size to Happyfield. In response to this increase, our community has seen a spike in citizen complaints about panhandling along with increases in petty crimes as reported by the local police department.

Strengths	◆ It provides the name of the applicant, name of town and the problem, and history of service.
	◆ It makes the reader want to learn more.
Weaknesses	◆ Listing the actual percentage of the increase, or if this is part of a trend of increases over the past few years, would add more value to an already strong draw.

Applicant 4

Sam is a forty-nine-year-old man without a permanent place to live for over five years. Twenty years ago, he was diagnosed with bipolar disorder and he has been in and out of treatment most of that time. When he lost his job over five years ago, he could no longer afford his medication, leading to unstable behavior that was outside the care his family could provide. Living on the streets was his only option and he is often seen begging for money so he can eat.

Sam's story is very similar to the approximately ten thousand estimated homeless individuals living on the streets of Happyfield. He would like to have a stable, predictable environment with the ability to control much of his life, but he is unable to adequately access the services he needs because he cannot come to a regular therapy appointment and find a doctor to stabilize him with medication and treatment. Many of the homeless individuals would choose otherwise if we were able to help them obtain short-term housing and treatment stabilization before moving on to a step-up program.

Strengths	◆ Compelling story catches the reader's heart.
Weaknesses	◆ It does not mention the name of the applicant.
	◆ The readers are not sure yet if the applicant is addressing the funder's stated need or if this application inadvertently went into the wrong "envelope," since there's no mention of the topic area.

The Need and Solution

This category is the heart of the case statement; this is where your energies should go when crafting a case statement. It requires a fine balance of credibility/logic/emotion, or ethos/logos/pathos. Often a writer will focus on one or two, and not include all three. This section should provide the reader with the big picture of, "Oh, I get the problem, understand what will fix it, and how Agency XYZ hopes to address and resolve it."

Every good need statement or case study will:

◆ Convey the need using credibility/logic/emotion (ethos/logos/pathos)

◆ Connect need with solution (cause ⇨ effect ⇨ solution)

◆ Identify/anticipate reasons for refusal

Elements of the Need and Solution

Here are some need and solution sections from the original applications. Let's see how they fared.

Applicant 1

Our community has two other organizations dealing with homelessness. One of them focuses on job opportunities and skill building, but does not address mental health issues. The other, which has very few beds available, only provides a soup kitchen, hands out gently used clothing, and opens its doors to allow homeless individuals to sleep during very poor weather conditions. In communities similar in size to ours, there are usually twice that many organizations and programs dealing with homelessness and many of them address issues of mental illness, a known contributing factor in this issue.

I'm Finally Home! has worked on the intersection of homelessness and mental illness for the past fifty years. Our long tradition makes us a staple in our community and a trusted provider. We have lacked the funds to provide a short-term stabilization program and the $90,000 would allow us to renovate a local home that was donated to us for this purpose and to get us started in providing this program for the first six months. During that time, we will be able to host fundraisers and enhance our billing to Medicaid for the mental health services.

Strengths	◆ It notes other programs and the gap in services.
	◆ It mentions the budget.
	◆ It mentions sustainability.

Weaknesses	◆ It's poorly written.
	◆ It provides no statistics.
	◆ It does not describe the program except that it is a temporary housing program with some undetermined services.

Applicant 2

The rate of homelessness in Happyfield is higher than in a nearby community and the state as a whole. Similarly, the rates of petty crime and citizen complaints about aggressive panhandling are also higher in our community, as seen in the table below. While we have three organizations addressing the homeless issue in our town, there is far more need than any of us can handle alone or together. The problems are simply too complex and diverse.

	Rate of Homelessness	Petty Crimes Reported	Aggressive Panhandling Reported
Happyfield	20.3	482	122
Sunnydale	15.2	261	65
State	16.8	922	342

We cannot say for sure what the link is between petty crime, aggressive panhandling, and homelessness. However, we have been tracking this information for the past ten years and the trends continue. By partnering with local hospitals and other community organizations, we can better address the myriad of issues around homelessness.

Strengths	◆ It used a table to present data.
Weaknesses	◆ If the cause of the problem is unclear, why state it?
	◆ The applicant describes what it does now as the solution. Supplanting rather than new programming?
	◆ It doesn't provide a clear cause-effect-solution.

Applicant 3

Numerous studies have shown that many individuals who are living on the streets often panhandle or commit petty crimes in order to get enough money for food. They also can be arrested for harassing citizens because of untreated mental health issues. The rates of homelessness in Happyfield are estimated to be 15 percent higher than in similar communities. Also, the rates of individuals with a mental health diagnosis are three times higher in our town compared to the state, according to the state board of behavioral health.

A recent study by the US Department of Health and Human Services demonstrated a strong link between untreated mental illness and homelessness. The cause has several factors including unstable treatment adherence, unstable medication adherence, and the lack of support from family. I'm Finally Home! will support up to fifty people per year with short-term housing in a *supportive environment for individuals who have a mental health diagnosis and who do not currently have stable housing. The $90,000 we are seeking will provide the seed money to provide ongoing support as they transition out of homelessness.*

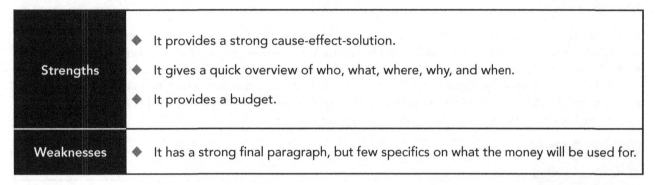

Strengths	◆ It provides a strong cause-effect-solution.
	◆ It gives a quick overview of who, what, where, why, and when.
	◆ It provides a budget.
Weaknesses	◆ It has a strong final paragraph, but few specifics on what the money will be used for.

Applicant 4

The homeless population in Happyfield is clearly linked to mental illness which is poorly addressed by the local social service organizations most likely due to lack of adequate funding and fragmented services. I'm Finally Home! have been addressing the behavioral health issues of our community with support services for over fifty years. As a leading organization we are well prepared to handle the intersection between homelessness and mental illness. Our rates of treatment plan adherence is within the top 10 percent of state.

The program will provide case management for up to forty clients per year who have the most unstable homeless issues. These are the individuals who are chronically homeless. This will lead to better stabilized living arrangements and better outcomes.

| Strengths | ◆ Mentions experience of the applicant; compares its statistics with the national average; lays out a program (but not sure if it's a new program). |
| Weaknesses | ◆ Weak cause-effect-solution, grammar issues, and, again, it's not clear if this is a new or existing program (supplanting?). The 10 percent percent statistic is weak. They are in the top 10 percent of *what*, exactly? |

In the above samples, Applicant 3 appears to be the only applicant who addresses cause-effect-solution. None of the examples demonstrates what the program might look like in even one or two sentences. Other than providing housing and case management, no real meat is given to the solution.

The Closing

The closing should be short and restate what has already been stated. It should give the reader confidence that your entity is capable of carrying out the goals and objectives of whatever endeavor it undertakes. It should:

◆ Forecast what will happen without the solution

◆ Repeat key ideas or statements

◆ Remind the reader why the applicant is the best choice

Now, let's take a look at the four applicants' closing statements and see if they address these three important elements.

Applicant 1

To sum up, the homeless population in Happyfield is linked closely to mental health issues. We believe that by addressing these needs, we will begin to reduce the homeless population. I'm Finally Home! will work with other providers to address this issue and the additional funds will support those efforts. Being homeless is not the ideal for anyone. Having a warm place to sleep and something to call their own will make the clients start to feel better even before they work closely with their caseworkers. Thank you for considering our proposal to help Happyfield be a better community.

Strengths	◆ Restated one of cause-effect-solutions and thanked the funder.
Weaknesses	◆ Hodge-podge of information with few details. The applicants also uses sweeping generalizations that may not resonate well with reviewers.

Applicant 2

I'm Finally Home! will provide a link to housing as well as case management and mental health services to our clients in an effort to reduce the homeless population in Happyfield. In helping to address the root causes of homelessness, we can chip away at the foundation of why we have so many homeless people in our community. By getting people into jobs and stable housing, we will also reduce petty crimes such as aggressive panhandling in our community. Our goals will be reached by helping clients get into a home they can call their own.

Strengths	◆ Gives a summary of activity.
Weaknesses	◆ No closing paragraph. A bit institution-centric, i.e., "Our goals will be reached by helping clients get into a home they can call their own."

Applicant 3

I'm Finally Home! is poised to address the needs of the homeless population because of our long history of providing mental health supports and case management services in this community. We consistently receive high satisfaction scores from our clients and our employee surveys rank their satisfaction very high as well. We know that strong employees who feel supported work hard for their clients. By providing the support services to the clients, we are getting to the causes of homelessness at the base, therefore adding to the likelihood that our clients will be successful in being able to find and keep stable housing.

The community of Happyfield will be strong and vibrant as we rally around those who need support the most. Our clients will be stronger also as we give them the tools they need to overcome their many hurdles to stabilization.

Strengths	◆ Gives a confident closing that speaks to the applicant's strengths and assets.
Weaknesses	◆ Doesn't acknowledge potential donor's role in meeting this need. Threw in an unrelated topic of employee satisfaction at the end with no data to support how it impacts the desired outcomes.

Applicant 4

For more than fifty years, I'm Finally Home! has worked to address the needs of the homeless in our community. We are confident that by targeting the mental health needs and providing support through case management, we can begin to reduce the numbers of individuals living on the streets of Happyfield. Every person who seeks our help will be given all of our energy to decrease the barriers that have kept these men and women in such dire straits. We appreciate the time and effort of the Foundation in considering this important request.

Strengths	◆ Restates the name of the entity, brings the focus to the beneficiaries, and thanks the funder.
Weaknesses	◆ Didn't mention the actual program by name.

It's possible that none of these applicants thought about the closing in terms of a logical sequence. Go back to some of your own case statements or letters of intent and compare your text against the suggested closing criteria.

Unlike the written prompt, time limits were not imposed on these submissions. To craft a case statement in ninety minutes requires the examinee to have internalized its key elements and the order of their presentation. The writer can then focus on making the case and incorporating the data provided in the written prompt instructions.

Consumer-centric vs. Institution-centric

A common mistake made by inexperienced grant developers is to talk about need in terms of *their* need. They will write about their programs and what their programs entail, and how funding will improve their programs, but overlook their greatest commodity—their consumers or the beneficiaries of their services. They will go on and on about the numbers served by their programs, and list outstanding personnel qualifications, but forget to bring it back to the target: the grant's beneficiaries and how their programs "change lives."

We recall a grant application requesting funding for a new parking lot for a community center. As justification for their need, the organization talked about the need for better handicap access, better night-time lighting for safety, improved drainage, and the ability to park 25 percent more cars. Absent from the need, though, was discussion of how the community center enhanced the lives of the beneficiaries, or the programming that would occur as a result of an improved facility. When asked about their grant application, they only half-jokingly said, "Well, you know it's awfully difficult to make an 'ask' for a parking lot 'sexy.' They clearly missed the point. A parking lot will never be 'sexy.'" It's the rare person who would fund a parking lot; people want to support people.

First-person Versus Third-person Voice

If only we could definitively answer the long-standing question of "Should I write in first person or in third person?" Everyone has an opinion and there is no definitive rule. Grant professionals, though, seem to follow this rule of thumb:

  ◆ If writing for private funding, use first person plural (as we're doing in this manual).

  ◆ If writing for public funding, use third person singular.

◆   If writing as an individual, use first person singular.

Some say that first person makes us seem real, as opposed to the more distant "it." Some say that first person can also sound needy or egocentric. If a study were taken to determine reader preferences regarding first person versus third person, we believe first person would be the voice of choice, since it feels more personal. However, in our opinion, the preferred go-to voice is third person, for a variety of reasons:

◆   Third person keeps the name of the entity up-close and memorable when reading a file cabinet full of new applications. There's nothing worse than having a reader say, "I liked that one grant application. What was the name of the organization again?"

◆   "We" statements can cause the reader to process "need" through the eyes of the service provider rather than the beneficiary. Third person may help direct the writer toward a need statement as seen through the eyes of the beneficiary, rather than the service provider.

◆   When we stop thinking about the grant in terms of "us," we move our story away from us and into the direction of beneficiaries and the subsequent impact.

Certainly, there is no clear answer as to the correct usage of voice. The above four text samples were written in both first and third person. Did a particular style resonate with you?

Letting the Funder Know That It, Too, Has a Need

In the late 1980s the government-funded Partnership for a Drug Free America issued a very memorable series of Public Service Announcements known as, "This is your brain on drugs." (Go ahead and google it—we'll wait. Be warned, it may forever change the way you think of eggs.)

This campaign also sparked RFPs from state departments of human services to fund health education programs about the dangers of drug and alcohol abuse. A community-based organization serving people who are deaf responded to this type of RFP, hoping to create a series of PSAs that were linguistically appropriate and culturally relevant to the Deaf community.

It opened its narrative with a full description of the PSA starring the ill-fated eggs. But then the narrative described a survey the organization completed with its own target population of twenty-seven people who are deaf that asked the question: "Have you seen this ad on TV?" Of this number, twenty-six said "no" and one person said: "Oh, yeah, I did. What's wrong with the egg?" How was this outcome possible? It was possible because the ad was not closed-captioned for deaf and hard-of-hearing viewers.

Public Service Announcement

While watching TV, one of the coauthors half-heartedly tuned in to a public service announcement (PSA) for a half-way house program for women being released from prison. Twelve hours later, this was the take-away from the clip:

The name of the program is Crossroads and the percentage of women who return to incarceration is 60 percent, compared to only 15 percent for women who complete the Crossroads program.

What caused the coauthor to finally pay attention to the PSA and focus on the message was the final reveal—the impact the program is having on beneficiaries, which in this case are the exoffenders and the society in which they live.

Did any of the sample case statements above speak of impact in this way?

stories from the real world

The rest of the proposal detailed the need in the more traditional way, sharing numbers and lack of services, as well as how funding the organization would be a "win-win" for not only the Deaf community but also the state department of health services. Clearly, putting the spotlight on the funder should be done carefully and with forethought, and with a quick return to the more traditional way of addressing need. However, at the time of this submission, it was the rare TV watcher who could not recall, "This is your brain; this is your brain on drugs." The grant reader and the funder could relate, and hopefully it planted the subtle seed of "who's really in need."

In this case, it was everyone: the Deaf community, the state department of health services, other future grantees that would also provide this health education, and society at large. By the way, the applicant was funded and given "high" marks for this approach. Did any of the above four texts use this strategy?

Persistence Trumps Ability, Every Time

Sometimes it takes persistence to win a grant award. We've all run into the funding source or grant opportunity we can't seem to win. We've tried the same project over and over, and we've tried a new more collaborative project year after year. We have provided more match and even asked for a third impartial party to read our proposal and provide feedback. Nothing seems to work.

Maybe your writing is good enough, the project is strong enough, your partners are good enough, the research is compelling enough, and the competition for scarce resources is too great. Maybe these are all true. Sometimes great grant proposals aren't selected for an award and the grant professional is not to blame.

Keep trying and don't give up. In our experience, persistence trumps ability, every time.

My Audience Isn't Me . . . or My Boss

Keep in mind that your true audience is not the person who signs your paychecks. For federal grants, your audience is most likely a peer group of reviewers—folks just like you with the same education level, employment background, and writing abilities. But what if your audience is a subcommittee of the foundation board, or a group of coworkers who were "vol-un-told" to show up on Saturday morning to read and score grant applications all day. How would you adjust your writing to reach a variety of audiences?

Instead, we recommend writing "to" an audience of one. For example, think about a lone subcommittee member reading the proposal at home after work. They might be getting paid a small stipend ($100 or less) for each proposal they read, but more than likely they're volunteers or they got volunteered. So they might be craving a little motivation. They will be reading to make sure you covered all the key points, for sure, and they'll be looking for something different, maybe even something creative. Make sure your proposal stands out from the rest. You don't need gimmicks, large bolded font, or colorful paper. Just write succinctly, use humor, and tell a story. You'll be glad you did and so will the reader!

In this chapter, we looked at the various strategies used by grant professionals to organize a clearly-stated case for funding. We've reviewed a common organizational structure used by professionals in the trenches; a structure organized around writing methodology that includes a "draw," "need and solution," and a "closing." If there's one take-away from this chapter beyond systematizing talking points within each category, it's the importance of crafting a case statement in terms of the beneficiary first and the organization second. And never lose sight of the goal of the case statement—to guide the reviewer into positive philanthropic space because of its belief in your need and your organization's solution.

Are You Exam Ready?

You are exam ready if you:

◆ Have a good internalization of the primary elements (talking points) that comprise a good case statement

◆ Have a clear picture of the *primary talking points* you want to address in a two- to three-page case statement

◆ Have a clear picture of the *order* in which you want to present those talking points in that case statement

◆ Have practiced writing a case statement within a ninety-minute timeframe

◆ Use Standard English

◆ Organize ideas appropriately and convey ideas clearly

◆ Can make a persuasive argument

Chapter Ten

Strategies to Reduce Test Anxiety

IN THIS CHAPTER

···→ Online test taking

···→ Have confidence in the multiple-choice and writing sample parts

···→ Dealing with stress and anxiety

···→ Celebrate like a grant professional!

The words "test," "quiz," or the dreaded phrase "this will be on the final exam" may conjure up painful memories of sweaty palms and racings hearts for most of us. If sitting for hours debating multiple-choice answers or solving word problems is how you unwind, stop reading now. Seriously, stop! You're making the rest of us very nervous!

Let's face it, most of us are not tested regularly, if at all, after we leave school. If you graduated a few years back, sitting for a professional credential exam may seem scary. But we're here for you! Each contributor to this manual chimed in with advice based on personal experience taking, and passing, the GPC. We've also included survey responses from other GPC participants who share their suggestions on how to reduce test anxiety. You've spent years learning how to succeed as a grant professional. Now we'll guide through some steps and activities to help you be best prepared to translate all that hard-won experience into crushing the GPC exam.

As a quick reminder, there are two parts to the GPC exam: the multiple-choice questions and the writing sample. In this chapter you'll find tips and tricks geared to each section.

Take a few minutes to assess your personal learning style. Do you like to be left alone with a user's manual, a superfast Wi-Fi connection, and a big cup of coffee to figure it all out? Or do you like to push aside any instructions, jump in, and learn by trial and error? You might be able to learn from others' mistakes or learn best after someone shows you how they did it. Many grant professionals learn about grants by attending training classes, conference workshops, and breakout sessions. Most of us learn best from conversing with colleagues, asking lots of questions, and reading every book we can find on the subject!

The point is that how you learn best can also help you best overcome test anxiety. Maybe reading scientific articles on stress reduction is your own personal panacea. Or maybe a quick call to a colleague who received a GPC will help you relax. If you're more of a "trial and error, seat of your pants, or let the chips fall where they may" kind of person, you may have already forgotten that you signed up to take the GPC exam.

Whoever you are, take the time to make sure you're in the best mental and physical state. Accept the fact that a few butterflies in the stomach are normal and may actually help you stay focused.

Knowing how you react to stress will help you determine which strategies will work best. If the idea of taking a test makes you physically ill, going for a jog or kickboxing might not be the best idea. Stressful situations can make people break out into hives, or make them so nervous they can't sleep for days. Think about what has worked for you in the past in stressful situations. Make a plan and stick with it.

Be aware that not all of our ideas for reducing test anxiety are included. Editors deleted a few (such as "chill out it's no big deal" and "don't worry, all grant professionals are good writers, right?") . . . with good reason!

Online Test Taking

For the first few years, all GPC exams were administered by volunteer proctors to groups of grant professionals at national and regional conferences and through local GPA chapters. Now you're able to take the GPC exams at any Kryterion testing center nationwide. The content didn't change, but there are a few key differences to consider. The first is that you'll be in a testing center, not in a hotel ballroom next door to a giant, boisterous wedding party. (Yes, this actually happened. No, we didn't catch the bouquet.) Second, the GPC exams are proctored by Kryterion test administrators who can't answer any questions the test taker has during the exam.

Multiple-choice Strategies

The multiple-choice section is just as important as the writing portion, as you'll need to pass both sections to get your GPC. When you first begin, read each question carefully before you start examining the possible answers. If you already know the answer first before seeing the multiple-choice responses, you're less likely to get thrown off track or tricked out of the correct answers.

Straight from the Painfully Obvious Department (POD), read *all* the choices before choosing your answer. Then eliminate answers you know are incorrect. Yes, it's common sense. But if you're anxious about taking a test, wouldn't you feel better with a concrete plan of attack in place before you even entered the testing center?

Try not to second-, third-, and fourth-guess yourself by changing your answer multiple times. Most likely your first choice is the right one, unless you misread the question.

Because as grant professionals we enjoy communicating in acronyms, here's another news flash from POD. In "All of the above" and "None of the above" choices, if you are certain one of the statements is true, don't choose "None of the above." Or, if one of the statements is false, don't choose "All of the above." You're welcome!

If you see at least two correct statements in a question with an "All of the above" choice, then "All of the above" is probably the answer. A positive choice is more likely to be true than a negative one. Usually the correct answer is the choice with the most information. But please remember that you're taking this exam because you are an experienced grant professional. You know this field, or you wouldn't be here in the first place. All the tips and tricks in the world cannot equal your own subject-matter expertise.

Writing under Timed Conditions

Time for true confessions! C'mon, under some crazy deadline pressure, we've dashed off proposals quicker than an undiscovered sequel to *Fast and Furious*. In an ideal world, you might prefer to draft narrative, put it away for a while, edit, and then have someone review it. We very much want to work in this ideal world, by the way! The good news is that if you've ever raced a ticking clock to meet an important proposal deadline, then you've already proven to yourself that you can write under timed conditions.

So pat yourself on the back, and then consider the following tips to help you focus quickly and efficiently on the writing section of the GPC. Read the writing prompt completely at least twice before typing the first word. This is where you will get the crucial information about the purpose and audience for the writing section. Remember the POD from a few paragraphs ago? It's back with news you can use; read and follow the directions! If there are spacing requirements, formatting requirements, or any other instructions, make yourself slow down and take them all in before your fingers hit the keyboard.

It may be tempting to start writing and get everything down at once, but try to at least outline the key points first. You don't want an ill-timed power surge to throw you off your writing game. If you've developed a brief schedule or planned an outline, you'll be able to stay focused. As you might have guessed, this is not the time to write the long-awaited sequel to *War and Peace*. Get to the point quickly and lead with specifics that help develop your persuasive arguments. Write clearly. Avoid jargon and acronyms. Use transition words and summarize in the last paragraph.

Finally, review, edit, and make corrections. Make sure you've followed all the instructions carefully. Proofread at least twice. Don't forget to follow all the instructions to submit your writing section.

Dealing with Stress and Anxiety

The better prepared you are for any exam, the less stress and anxiety you will feel. We recommend learning about your stressors, understanding how you react, and taking the steps you can to control your anxiety levels. A certain amount of stress and anxiety is healthy; both mean that you are a professional concerned about your career. Stress and anxiety levels that prevent you from taking or doing well on your exam are not healthy.

Here are some strategies you can try before exam day:

- ◆ Visit the exam or site location in advance (if possible).

- ◆ Get to bed early the night before and avoid alcohol, and before that . . . .

- ◆ Eat "calming" foods such as fresh fruit and tree nuts.

- ◆ Avoid "stressful" foods such as sugary, high-carb, junk, or highly processed snacks.

Make a call to your BFF, throw your dog a ball, play a guitar, watch a rom-com, or read a magazine or a grant blog. If you make a plan and either follow some of the suggested strategies or develop ones that work best for you, you will feel more in control of your own emotions. Remember, it's normal to feel a little nervous. Try not to dwell on it, and use your feelings to help you stay focused.

The strategy for the day of and during the exam should be different. You certainly can't play your guitar or listen to music during the exam! So don't over-eat the day of the exam. Eat a light or balanced meal beforehand. Use your favorite relaxation techniques, especially meditation. At the start of the exam, remember to stay focused on one question at a time, and don't get ahead of yourself. Always do your best, but don't expect perfection. You just need to pass! No one will ever learn your score.

Celebrate like a Grant Professional!

When grant professionals celebrate, it's usually about grant awards or reports submitted on time. The happiest cubicle dance occurs when the grant closeout letter arrives! We've all seen professional football players celebrate a touchdown by spiking the football and performing an impossible back flip. Celebrate that the exam is done!

Every grant professional is different, and we expect every celebration to be different, too. We may celebrate by enjoying a long weekend away or well-deserved vacation! Share a meal with friends at your favorite restaurant or a night out with your spouse! Indulge in your guilty pleasure snacks (like chocolate, potato chips, or ice cream) or watch TV! Spending time with family can be relaxing and so can reading a good book.

We know your experience and knowledge as an active grant professional has prepared you well for the GPC exam. One of the most important factors for success on the exam is that you've met the prerequisites. If GPCI accepted your application, you have the years of experience, the number of grants awarded, and the education to become a GPC. The examination is the last step in the credentialing process.

We hope this book was helpful to you and either confirmed what you already knew about grants or served to fill in any gaps in your experience and skills. Tell us how you did!

Good luck!

We Surveyed Recent GPCs!

To get some real world perspective, the Grant Professionals Foundation surveyed and interviewed more than fifty GPC recipients. Recent GPC recipients shared the following information about online test taking and the Kryterion testing centers:

◆ The testing centers can be chilly—take a sweater or a jacket.

◆ It can take a few minutes to sign in, so arrive early to the testing center on the day of your exam.

◆ The computers at the testing centers may or may not have spell check—plan on not having it.

◆ Computer issues and power surges are possible, so be prepared to wait and be patient.

Apparently, online test taking is a dish best served cold!

 **stories from the real world**

Appendix A

Authors' Recommended Reading List

The Authors' Recommended Reading List is a collection of our favorite books. Here are our recommendations for prep manuals and guides, accounting (for grants), fundraising, grants, project management, and program evaluation.

GPC Prep Manual/Guide

The GPA Bookstore offers for sale a GPC Prep Guide developed by the Broward County local chapter of GPA. This book is a guide that should be used in conjunction with this GPC refresher manual.

Christine Heft, Shelia McCann, Jodi Pearl, Susan Webster and Amy Whitlock. *Study Guide & Annotated Bibliography: Support for the Grant Professional Certification Examination*, 2nd ed. Grant Professionals Association: Broward County Florida Chapter, 2011.

Accounting (for Grants)

Grant accounting is a unique form of accounting. Nonprofits and governments alike are held to certain accounting standards only accountants really understand. Grant professionals need to know the basics.

Steven M. Bragg. *Generally Accepted Accounting Principles (GAAP) Guidebook: 2015 Edition*. Accounting Tools Publishing, 2014.

M. Letha Daniels. *Grant Management Non-Profit Fund Accounting: For Federal, State, Local and Private Grants Getting Started—Setting Up and Tracking Grants*. Blessings Abound LLC: Kindle Edition, 2015.

Joanne M. Flood. Wiley GAAP 2015: *Interpretation and Application of Generally Accepted Accounting Principles*. Wiley Regulatory Reporting. New York: Wiley, 2014.

Laurence Scot. *The Simplified Guide to Not-for-Profit Accounting, Formation and Reporting*. New York: Wiley, 2010.

Fundraising

Fundraising is similar and related to grant seeking. Both are a form of development. Not all fundraising is grant seeking. A nonprofit engages in fundraising by seeking donations, resources, and grants. Some grant professionals are excellent fundraisers.

Meredith Hancks. *Getting Started in Prospect Research: What You Need to Know to Find Who You Need to Find.* In the Trenches Series: CharityChannel Press, 2011.

Meredith Hancks and Cara Rosson. *Fundraising Research Made Easy: A Practical Guide for Fundraisers.* In the Trenches Series: CharityChannel Press, 2013.

Susan Black. *Help! They Want Me to Fundraise! A Nonprofit Fundraising Manual for Beginners.* In the Trenches Series: CharityChannel Press, 2014.

Linda Lysakowski. *Fundraising for the GENIUS (Second Edition).* For the GENIUS Series: For the GENIUS Press, an Imprint of CharityChannel LLC, 2014.

Grants

Grant seeking is a form of development like fundraising. Grant awards are usually the result of a grant application, submitted for consideration to a grantmaking foundation or government agency.

Goodwin Deacon and Ken Ristine. *Grantsmanship for the GENIUS.* For the GENIUS Series: For the GENIUS Press, an Imprint of CharityChannel LLC, 2016.

Cheryl Kester and Karen Cassidy. *Writing to Win Federal Grants: A Must-Have for Your Fundraising Toolbox.* In the Trenches Series: CharityChannel Press, 2015.

Cheryl Kester and Karen Cassidy. *Writing to Win Federal Grants—The Workbook.* In the Trenches Series: CharityChannel Press, 2015.

Relaxation Techniques!

If you make a plan and either follow some of the suggested strategies or develop ones that work best for you, you'll feel more in control of your own emotions. These relaxation techniques might work for you to reduce stress:

◆ Meditation

◆ Deep breathing

◆ Mindfulness

◆ Listen to music

◆ Exercise

◆ Yoga

◆ Visualization

◆ Stop and have a cup of tea or coffee

◆ Take a break from studying and go outside

◆ Pick your own way to de-stress (play a video game, do some research, or check your emails)

Michael Wells. *Strategic Grantsmanship: It's Time to Raise Your Game.* In the Trenches Series: CharityChannel Press, 2015.

Joanne Oppelt. *Confessions of a Successful Grants Writer: A Complete Guide to Discovering and Obtaining Funding.* In the Trenches Series: CharityChannel Press, 2011.

Kimberly Richardson. *The Official Federal Grants Prep Guide: 10 Tips to Position Your Organization for Success.* Kearney, Nebraska: Morris Publishing, 2013.

Project Management

Project management is a systematic method for implementing any number of projects or programs. Projects may receive all or part of their funds from a grant award.

Glen B. Alleman. *Performance-Based Project Management: Increasing the Probability of Project Success.* New York: AMACOM Publisher, 2014.

John C. Goodpasture. *Quantitative Methods in Project Management.* Plantation, Florida: J. Ross Publishing, 2003.

Kathy Schwalbe. *An Introduction to Project Management, Fifth Edition. With Brief Guides to Microsoft Project 2013.* Schwalbe Publishing, 2015.

Robert K. Wysocki. *Effective Project Management: Traditional, Agile, Extreme*, 7th ed. New York: Wiley, 2013.

Program Evaluation

Many grant applications require or allow for program evaluations. The evaluator can determine if the program or grant project is performing well or making an impact.

David Royse, Deborah K. Padgett, Bruce A. Thyer, and T.K. Logan. *Program Evaluation: An Introduction*, 5th ed. Independence, Kentucky: Cengage Learning, 2009.

Joseph S. Wholey, Harry P. Hatry, and Kathryn E. Newcomer. *Handbook of Practical Program Evaluation*, 3rd ed. New York: Wiley, 2010.

David R. Black, Elizabeth S. Foster, and Judith A. Tindall. *Evaluation of Peer and Prevention Programs: A Blueprint for Successful Design and Implementation.* New York: Routledge, 2011.

Appendix B

GPCI Literature Review

GPCI does not promote any specific study guide related to the exam. However, GPCI has published a GPCI Literature Review. It is posted on its website at *http://bit.ly/gpci-literature-review.*

The GPCI Literature Review may be helpful to GPC candidates looking to refresh knowledge or fill experience gaps in the grant field. This review contains general grant information as well as a list of books, journal articles, and websites that may be of interest.

Michael Wells, author and grant consultant, originally prepared the GPCI Literature Review (2006) as a tool in developing the credentialing examination and has recently (2011) updated it for use by grant professionals who wish to refresh their knowledge prior to taking the exam.

Index

If you enjoyed this workbook, you'll want to pick up *Writing to Win Federal Grants: A Must-Have for Your Fundraising Toolbox*, published by CharityChannel Press as part of the popular **In the Trenches**™ series for nonprofit-sector practitioners.

IN THE Trenches™

Writing to Win Federal Grants

A Must-Have for Your Fundraising Toolbox

Cheryl L. Kester, CFRE
Karen L. Cassidy, GPC

Master federal grants by learning how to:

- Create compelling need statements and budgets
- Design detailed projects for more competitive proposals
- Assemble proposal development teams and effective partnerships
- Step up your game by developing evaluation plans suited to federal grants

Multiple examples from successful proposals demonstrate these concepts in action.

CharityChannel.com/bookstore

*Charity*Channel
PRESS™

And don't forget to pick up the companion workbook, *Writing to Win Federal Grants: The Workbook.*

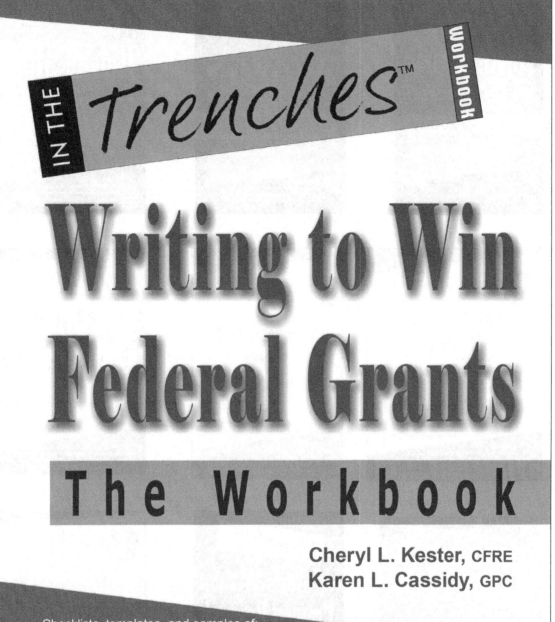

IN THE **Trenches**™ Workbook

Writing to Win Federal Grants
The Workbook

Cheryl L. Kester, CFRE
Karen L. Cassidy, GPC

Checklists, templates, and samples of:

■ The most commonly used federal forms with annotations
■ Multiple styles of logic models, MOUs, and letters of support
■ Tools to rate RFAs and assess organizational readiness to apply
■ Four complete federal proposals with notes and tips from the authors

And so much more!

CharityChannel.com/bookstore

*Charity*Channel
PRESS™

If you enjoyed this book, you'll want to pick up the other books in the CharityChannel Press **In the Trenches™** series.

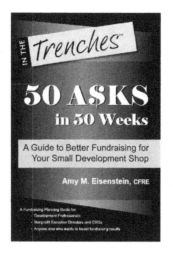

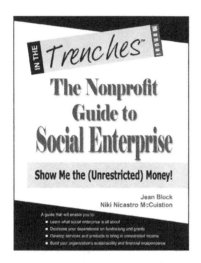

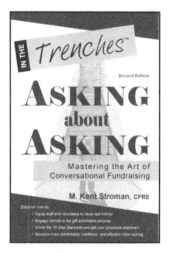

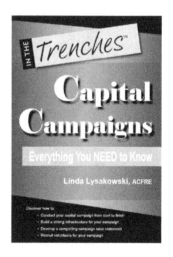

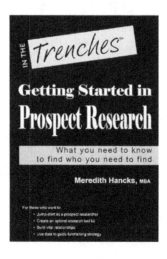

CharityChannel.com/bookstore

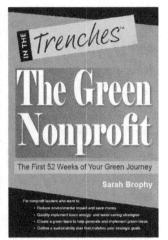

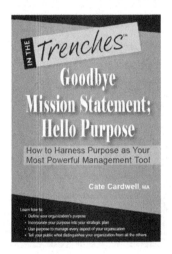

CharityChannel.com/bookstore

In the Trenches™

The Nonprofit Consulting Playbook

Winning Strategies from 25 Leaders in the Field

Edited by:
Susan Schaefer, CFRE
Linda Lysakowski, ACFRE

The first book of its kind to:
- Delve into consultants' firsthand experiences
- Help new consultants get started on the right foot
- Reveal veterans' strategies for reinventing themselves
- Expose mishaps and lessons learned from some of the field's best

In the Trenches™

The Leaky Bucket

What's Wrong with Your Fundraising and How You Can Fix It

Ellen Bristol
Linda Lysakowski, ACFRE

Learn how to:
- Use metrics to measure your fundraising programs
- Develop an infrastructure for your development office
- Assess what you've been doing wrong and learn how to fix it

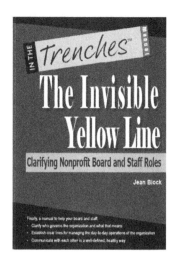

In the Trenches™

The Invisible Yellow Line

Clarifying Nonprofit Board and Staff Roles

Jean Block

Finally, a manual to help your board and staff:
- Clarify who governs the organization and what that means
- Establish clear lines for managing the day-to-day operations of the organization
- Communicate with each other in a well-defined, healthy way

In the Trenches™

Fundraising for Schools

8 Keys to Success Every Head of School Should Know

Linda Wise McNay, PhD

A guide that will help you:
- Learn the secrets to fundraising success
- Prepare your school for a capital campaign
- Raise funds for your school with step-by-step instruction
- Find out how much time the head of school should devote to fundraising

In the Trenches™

Raise More Money from Your Business Community

A Practical Guide to Tapping into Corporate Charitable Giving

Linda Lysakowski, ACFRE

Raise more money for your nonprofit organization by:
- Identifying the types of businesses likely to give
- Communicating with business leaders in a more compelling manner
- Involving volunteers from the business world in your fundraising activities

In the Trenches™

Moving Up to Executive Director

Lessons Learned from My First 365 Days

Joanne Oppelt, MHA, GPC

A guide for:
- Transitioning to the corner office
- Preparing for your executive director role
- Handling your first year as a new executive director

In the Trenches™

YOU and Your Nonprofit Board

Advice and Practical Tips from the Field's Top Practitioners, Researchers, and Provocateurs

Edited by:
Terrie Temkin, PhD

The first governance book of its kind to:
- Reexamine governance at its source
- Challenge dogma about the board versus chief executive roles
- Let YOU decide if you still agree with the old thinking on governance
- Take aim at myths about governance that hold organizations back
- Provide practical, in-the-trenches advice and tips you can use NOW

In the Trenches™

Confessions of a Successful Grants Writer

A Complete Guide to Discovering and Obtaining Funding

Joanne Oppelt, MHA, GPC

A Guide for:
- Grant Writers
- Development Professionals
- Foundation, Corporate and Government Relationship Professionals
- Anyone Wanting to Raise More Revenue through Proposals

In the Trenches™

Fundraising for Museums

8 Keys to Success Every Museum Leader Should Know

Linda Wise McNay, PhD

A guide that will help you:
- Learn the secrets to fundraising success
- Prepare your museum for a capital campaign
- Assist with your museum's membership techniques
- Find out how much time a museum leader should devote to fundraising

CharityChannel.com/bookstore

Charity Channel
PRESS™

And now introducing **For the GENIUS® Press,** an imprint that produces books on just about any topic that people want to learn. You don't have to be a genius to read a **GENIUS** book, but you'll sure be smarter once you do!

ForTheGENIUS.com/bookstore

Just Published!

Casino
Video Poker
for the GENIUS®

Take the mystery out of
video poker and boost
your casino fun!

Linda G. Nowell

FOR THE GENIUS IN ALL OF US™

ForTheGENIUS.com/bookstore

PRESS

Just Published!

ForTheGENIUS.com/bookstore

Made in the USA
Las Vegas, NV
16 November 2024

11892806R00092